Advance Praise for
Organizing the Disorganized Child

"A superb book! Blessedly brief, pointedly practical, and clear as glass, this book will help any child, parent, or teacher who reads it. Step by step, the authors, who truly know their subject, lead the reader through a method that can't help but succeed. This book meets an urgent need. I will be referring it to my patients." —EDWARD HALLOWELL, MD, coauthor of *Driven to Distraction* and *Superparenting for ADD*

"*Organizing the Disorganized Child* is a long overdue manual that strives to make life easier on families with children with ADHD. Unlike other books that offer a menu of one-size-fits-all strategies, this book digs deeper and helps parents to understand the root causes of their particular child's disorganization. . . . This book is a MUST HAVE for all parents of children with or without ADHD RATEY, author of *organized Mind*

"By revealing how the fault of the parents, the teach to do with how the frontal lobes of the bra will guide us to much more constructive solutions." —ELLEN GALINSKY, president of the Families and Work Institute

"You will wear out your highlighter! Not only is this book full of easy-to-understand, detailed directions to help you organize your child while in school, if you use the suggested strategies you will be teaching them lifelong invaluable skills. I will be recommending this book to all parents of kids with ADHD." —HEIDI BERNHARDT, national director, Centre for ADHD Advocacy Canada

"*Organizing the Disorganized Child* is a breath of fresh air. Straightforward, practical and most important providing strategies and ideas that any parent—even the disorganized—can easily implement. Rather than wait till some children struggle, I suggest that *Organizing the Disorganized Child* be essential reading for parents of all entering first graders." —SAM GOLDSTEIN, PH.D., coauthor of *Raising a Self-Disciplined Child*

"Get out your yellow highlighter! *Organizing the Disorganized Child* delivers on its promise to teach a child or student better organization and study skills. In addition to describing the 'why' behind the behaviors of so many kids with weak planning and execution skills—you know, the ones so quickly labeled as 'lazy' or 'disinterested'—authors Kutscher and Moran present page after page of creative, commonsense ideas that work!" —VERONICA ZYSK, managing editor, *Autism-Asperger's Digest Magazine* and coauthor of *1001 Great Ideas for Teaching and Raising Children with Autism Spectrum Disorders*

"At last! A survival manual for any parent, teacher, or therapist who asks, 'How on earth can I help this child get organized—and stay that way?' Born of the authors' real-life experiences and professional expertise, this guide mercifully spares you the abstract theories and yet more talk of color-coded folders, leading you into the land of Strategies that Work. Practical, smart, and entertaining." —GINA PERA, author of *Is It You, Me, or Adult ADD?*

"This practical 'how-to' book is an invaluable tool to help parents effectively guide their children in the development of organizational skills. The authors have translated their impressive expertise, wisdom, and insights into a remarkably comprehensive and refreshingly direct step-by-step approach." —BARBARA FIRESTONE, PH.D., president and CEO of The Help Group

"Wow! Easy to read and practical, too! Dr. Kutscher and Ms. Moran have indeed taken the stress out of dealing with a disorganized child and made family life a whole lot more manageable. *Organizing the Disorganized Child* is packed with plenty of how-to strategies, lists, and other concrete suggestions to deal with issues ranging from getting your child out of the house in the morning to buying notebooks and backpacks. I highly recommend it for all struggling students and their overwhelmed parents." —PATRICIA O. QUINN, MD, director, Center for Girls and Women with ADHD

Organizing the Disorganized Child

Organizing

the Disorganized

Child

Simple Strategies to Succeed in School

MARTIN L. KUTSCHER, M.D.

and

MARCELLA MORAN, M.A., L.M.H.C.

harperstudio

An Imprint of HarperCollins*Publishers*

This information is presented for educational purposes only. It does not constitute medical advice, nor a therapeutic relationship between the authors and the reader.

FIRST EDITION

Designed by Jennifer Daddio/Bookmark Design & Media Inc.

Library of Congress Cataloging-in-Publication Data has been applied for.

ISBN 978-0-06-179741-5

09 10 11 12 13 WBC/RRD 10 9 8 7 6 5 4 3 2 1

To my wife and children,
who have taught me so much.
—MK

To my family, especially my children,
Ian and Ava,
for their patience and support.
—MM

Contents

Organizing the Disorganized Child

Introduction

"Does he use his assignment book? Are you kidding!?!? He doesn't even know where it is. He never plans ahead. We're always going back to school to get the right books. At home, I have to stay with him or nothing gets accomplished. And then—after we fight for hours to get the homework done—he forgets to hand it in the next morning! Our whole family is at wit's end. When will the fighting stop?"

We, too, are parents of children who struggle with organizational skills. We've heard the reports that the kids are bright but need to apply themselves. We've been up late at night, gluesticking that poster project that was assigned two weeks ago but that we just found out about. We've experienced the frustration, anger, and hopeless feelings that can arise when dealing with a disorganized child. We've been through all of the fighting.

In our professions as a pediatric neurologist (Martin) and a therapist/coach (Marcella), we have used these experiences to guide our work with children who have problems with organization, homework, and study skills. Most of their parents are completely stressed out by the time they make it to us. Many families have turned to the school or therapists for help. As we've discovered, though, the school and the therapists often don't have the skills, the know-how, or the time to solve the problems. *Organizing the Disorganized Child* shows parents how to take the reins and teach organizational and study skills to their children. It puts the situation back in control.

This book finally will answer the parents' question "How can I help my child get organized without it being a fight?" Other books offer some strategies, take into account the learning style of the child, and even give resources as to where you can buy clear plastic boxes to store junk. But this book is the essential organizational guide that factors organizational styles into the equation and offers effective strategies that deliver amazing long-term results. We will show not only parents but also teachers, schools, counselors, coaches, and therapists a simple set of personalized organizing and study skills to teach to children so that they can experience all the success they deserve.

A common pitfall of many approaches is the belief that we simply need to *show* kids how to be organized. "Look!" Mom says. "I showed him a few times how to use a planner. He's fixed now. Phew!" If it were quite that easy, we'd be done in an hour. We're not going to fall into that trap. Late elementary and middle school kids likely already know how to use a planner—it's not that tough to learn. If you were to give them a true/false quiz on using an agenda book, they'd probably get a 100 percent. Try it. Ask your

child a few questions: "You should write down all of your assignments: true or false? You should check assignments off when they
are completed: true or false?" See! They already know *what* to do.
What they can't do is actually *do* it. That's because some people
have a problem actually carrying out (executing) their intentions.

Thus, teaching children with organizational difficulties what
to do is often useless unless you can ensure that there's an organizational system in place to oversee the execution of those skills.
The parents and teachers need to know more than just how to
teach a child the appropriate organizational techniques. They
must also be taught how to provide ongoing supervision of these
skills at the moment that help is actually needed—not punishment after the child has already underperformed. So *Organizing
the Disorganized Child* explains both how to teach and how to supervise organizational skills.

Making sure students are organized enough to know what
they are supposed to do is a great, necessary start. However, they
still need to read, take notes, and study the material. Some students effortlessly learn these skills. However, many just don't have
a clue. This book will help caregivers teach these learning skills to
all of those students who haven't absorbed the techniques through
osmosis.

So, what is the step-by-step game plan? Chapter 1 explains the
roots of our children's organizational problems and the parents'
role in fixing them. Chapter 2 explains the different organizational styles used by different students. Not all kids organize the
same way! We'll build upon these insights in the rest of the book.
In chapter 3, we'll discuss what materials to buy and how to set up
the study area. Chapter 4 lays out a step-by-step plan for an organizational system. We'll follow the paper trail: getting the correct

work home, planning the work, and getting it back to where it belongs. Chapter 5 explains to parents how to teach their children reading, note-taking, study, and test-taking skills. Chapter 6 will address organizing the morning and nighttime routines. In the appendices, we'll address some of the conditions that might be causing the organizational problems, such as ADHD or learning disabilities, and give suggestions for further readings.

Some techniques will result in rapid change. Even just a few pointers can deliver meaningful results. One key, for example, is to make the material more meaningful by teaching the student to constantly ask him/herself questions about what is being read, written, or studied. This key technique of asking questions often results in a deeper and clearer understanding of the material. However, not all brains are preprogrammed for good organizational and study skills. We can't completely fix everything overnight. We can, though, expect continued progress over a mountainous terrain toward an ultimately successful future. The fighting will stop!

Let's get started!

Chapter 1

How Did My Child Get So Disorganized? (And How Do I Start Fixing It?)

"I don't really blame Judy's teachers for thinking that she doesn't care about school. If I didn't love her so much, I wouldn't believe that she cared, either. But I know that she is such a good kid! She's aware that she has to do the work. Yet she keeps sabotaging herself. She comes home and invariably is missing some of her assignments— and doesn't even know it. Then we spend hours fighting to get it done. (It would be so much faster if I could just do it for her. Frankly, I just did a great job on her poster project! We got an A!) We finally get homework done, and then she can't find it in the morning when her teacher asks for it! The teacher thinks that she's lazy, but I know that if she were really lazy, she wouldn't have done it in the first place. After all, once she's done it, she may as well hand it in for the credit. How can she be so smart at coming up with ideas for her paper and so, well . . . dumb when it comes to handing it in? I just don't get it!

"Fortunately, I came across this great idea: We now have a separate folder for all homework to be handed in. When any teacher asks for the homework, there's only one place she has to look—in that folder. And I know it's there, because I double-checked it last night. Simple solution. Problem solved. On to the next issue."

How Did My Child Get into This Mess?

Some kids are naturally organized. Heaven bless them. If you are reading this book, your child probably isn't one of them. So, what happened? Who is to blame?

We're really not into blame. We just want to fix the problem. However, understanding the root cause of the disorganization does guide our efforts to fix it. So, if we must assign blame, then it falls to a child's frontal lobes. The fault is not the parents' or the teachers'. The fault does not lie in the child's willfulness. It's the brain. Understanding that it's nobody's fault allows us to cut through the counterproductive blame game. It allows us to stop feeling like victims of a "lazy child" or an "uncaring teacher" and focus instead on working together to teach and finesse the child's brain— which is still in the process of being formed until young adulthood. That slow brain development was probably okay in simpler times. Now, though, society expects so much more planning from our children, and so much sooner.

So let's take a paragraph or two to explain why your child's brain has trouble with organization. It turns out that our organizational skills come from a part of the brain called the frontal lobes—conveniently located in the front of our head, just behind our forehead. Go ahead. Touch the area. These frontal lobes are responsible for getting things accomplished.

According to *Taking Charge of ADHD* by R. A. Barkley, frontal lobe skills allow us to:

- *stop paying attention to trivial, albeit fascinating, things* (such as paper clips on the desk). Scientists call this skill of filtering out distractions "inhibition."
- *prepare for what is coming up in the future* (such as two papers both due finals week). This is called "foresight."
- *remember what happened the last time* we didn't remember what was coming up in the future (such as when we didn't write those papers in advance and tried to write them both the night before they were due). This skill is called "hindsight."
- *make a step-by-step plan for the future* (such as "I'll read the book for the first paper this week and write the paper next week"). This is called "planning."
- *figure out how long each step of the plan is going to take*, i.e., have a "concept of time." Many kids really think that they can write a ten-page paper (and take a shower) in one night, no matter how many times it hasn't worked before. It's not just procrastination. It's a poor concept of time, a brain-based skill.
- *talk to ourselves as we make the plan*, a skill called "self-talk" which is necessary for effective problem solving.
- *juggle simultaneously the pros and cons about that plan*—i.e., use "working memory."
- *flexibly alter the plan* as circumstances change (and they will).

- *actually start, carry out, and complete the plan* (not just have the best of intentions), called "execution."
- repeat for the next class subject.

And we expect children to be capable of these "executive functions" by the end of middle school—long before their frontal lobes are actually fully developed. If the students are not capable of these functions on their own, then we expect that demoralizing F's will somehow magically teach these skills to them.

In addition to these biological factors, society places a lot of demands on our kids these days, not just limited to school academics; there are clubs, sports, dance, theater, get-togethers, community service, Facebook, e-mail, instant messaging, video games, TV, family time, dinner, shopping, and hygiene—all to be completed in time to catch a few hours of sleep, so that they can start it all over again tomorrow. And they haven't even hit high school yet.

. . . .

It's not the child's fault that his brain has not yet fully developed. He doesn't want to be disorganized or get bad grades any more than you want him to. Demoralizing F's will not magically teach him the needed skills.

. . . .

In short, the brains of many kids have not yet matured fully enough to meet the amazing increased demands of our society. It's not the children's fault. They don't want the bad grades any more than you do.

What Didn't Cause This Mess?

Laziness.

We've looked through the index of every book that we have on child development, child behavior, and child neurology. "Laziness" is not there. We checked under U for "unmotivated." Nothing there, either. Laziness and lack of motivation are not diagnoses. They are not the root problem. I doubt that any child with a typically functioning brain and a supportive environment ever says to herself, "I could do well and get A's and praise. Or I could blow off my work and get yelled at. Gee, I'd rather choose the option of getting punished. That sounds like so much fun!"

Certainly, after years of difficulty with school and homework, some kids have learned to not even try anymore. After all, they already know that schoolwork doesn't come readily to them, so why bother this year? But they didn't start out lazy (just remember their kindergarten years!), and they aren't lazy now . . . just beaten down. We've got to teach them the skills to get unstuck. That's what this book will help you do.

Remember: They are not lazy; they are disorganized!

Why Don't They Know How to Read, Take Notes, or Study?

Why do so many kids fail to master academic skills naturally? Well, why shouldn't they? These skills are not hardwired into our children's brains. Evolution didn't prepare them for these tasks.

Our brains are hardwired for eating, sleeping, finding a mate, and talking. There are no hardwired parts of the brain for academic skills such as underlining key concepts while you read. Although some children seem to learn these techniques by simple observation or osmosis, many don't. Often, the students don't learn them well in school. This book will help parents explicitly teach these skills to their children. Even kids who have mastered many of the basics will still benefit from refining their skills with techniques from this text.

The Parents' Role

Three quick questions:

1. Who bought this book, you or your child?
2. Who is the one who consciously recognizes that there is a problem?
3. Who is going to have to bring up this topic?

Answer to questions 1–3: (Do you really need us to tell you?) You, the parents.

You. Yes, you. But don't freak out. You've already come a long way. You recognize that your child needs help. You recognize that yelling doesn't work, and you've taken the step of buying a book to look for alternative solutions to punishment. You are already light-years ahead of the game. Congratulations! Now, let's talk about your role in bringing up the topic of organization and in supervising your child until the necessary skills become ingrained.

> You've already made a major step. Seriously. You recognize that your child needs help, and you're ready for some new approaches other than yelling.

Bringing Up the Topic with Your Child

We suspect that your child already senses that *something* is wrong. She already knows that her grades aren't very good. She already knows that she is fighting with her parents over homework and incomplete assignments. She already is resentful that there isn't enough free time. One child told us, "I'm tired of not being able to find things when I need them, and finding them when I don't!" So this topic is not likely to be earth-shattering news to your child. In fact, a calm conversation about the issue might even come as a relief— she will certainly feel better about it than she would about being yelled at again. The keys to successfully introducing the topic of organization are to stay calm, listen to your child, and stay positive.

Stay Calm!

Broach the topic when everyone is calm and there are no other pressing issues on anyone's mind. Do *not* bring this up when either you or the child is already about to lose it—or, even worse, already in the middle of a fight. No, you need all of your child's (and your own) problem-solving skills to be available during these discussions. As R. W. Greene established in *The Explosive Child*, inflamed frontal lobes can't think clearly. What are the odds that your screaming child will suddenly stop and politely say, "Mom, come to think of it, I like your idea on how I could improve my life"? Similarly, a child who is currently focused on a different pressing issue, such as getting to the store for his new cleats, will not be able to get past that problem in order to work on a new topic. Typically, finding such a calm moment will require making an appointment with your child—at a mutually agreeable time. A quick pointer: When your child is in the middle of looking at something with a screen, it is not a good time for a calm, meaningful conversation.

Have discussions only when calm. What are the odds that your screaming child will suddenly stop to say, "Mom, come to think of it, I like your idea on how I could improve my life"? Typically, finding such a calm moment will require making an appointment with your child.

At the appointed time, bring up the topic in a nonaccusatory, empathic fashion. This is not about reprimand or punishment. "Johnny, I've noticed we've been fighting a lot about your schoolwork. I'm not feeling good about us arguing, and I can't imagine that you feel good about it, either. Can we talk about making things better? I want to listen. What isn't working for you? How can we work out a solution? You might not even know what is or isn't working for you and that's okay. We'll figure this out together."

A child who is angry or skeptical may resist your help at first. This may partly be due to fear that you will call his teacher and really bring attention to him. Realize that if the teacher hasn't contacted you yet, your child been skating under the radar, just where he likes it. Propose some mutual boundaries you both agree on, such as giving him the chance to act independently and assertively in approaching his teacher for extra help. If he does not follow through, you will need to step in and call the teacher to set up an appointment. However, you *must* give him the opportunity to act first.

Remind the child of the benefits of being organized:

* Homework gets done faster
* More free time for activities such as sports or video games
* Less yelling in the house
* Fewer punishments
* Less frustration
* Better grades
* And did we mention, more free time and less yelling?

Actually Listen to Your Child!

"I tell you all the time, Mom—studying from flash cards does not work for me! That only worked for you when you were a student."

It's hard for us to believe that the strategies that have been so successful for us may not work for our child, but they may not. We hear kids say all the time, "That may work for you, Mom. It makes sense, but it doesn't work for me."

Important! Listen to your child!

So how do we find what will work? Start by listening to your child. If nothing else, your child can teach you what doesn't work for her. Listen. Listen. Listen. We don't usually do that. Usually, we cut her off or dismiss her ideas. After all, we're the parents. We know what's best, right? (Quick reality check: Think back to all the times your child said that a certain technique didn't work for her. Do you remember any details of what she said? Did you really listen to her? Don't feel bad if you didn't.)

This time, you're going to listen and take what you hear into account as you work through this book.

Stay Positive

How would you like it if your boss constantly criticized you? Would you find yourself motivated and energized to do your best? When the door opened and your boss's face appeared, would you be glad? Would you look forward to having dinner with your critical boss? Would you want to discuss the topic of organization with him?

If you want to bring out your child's self-motivation—and preserve your relationship with him—you'll need to keep it positive. Punishments don't teach skills.

So keep it positive. Find something to praise. Use humor to redirect a deteriorating interaction. If there is a punishment that needs to be handed out, do it without a nasty attitude. Since punishments don't teach skills anyway, make them short and to the point. Then figure out a way to durably fix the problem so it won't happen again. (That's why you're reading this book.)

Always remember that there is a real live child—yours—under that disorganized mess.

Remember, this is not war. Neither the child nor the parent is the enemy. They are teammates in this mess, together. The winner is the family that stays together. The techniques of staying calm, listening to your child, and keeping it positive are ongoing strategies for all of your interactions.

Someone Needs to Keep Supervising These Skills

The rest of this book will help you and your child determine his organizational style and apply that knowledge to a doable system of organization and study skills. However, you usually can't just teach these skills once and be done with it. If that approach had worked, you wouldn't still be having problems. So why didn't teaching it once "fix" the problem? It's because many kids' frontal lobes have trouble carrying out the plan. They know what to do; they just can't *do* it. So someone (hint: Who's reading this book?) will have to lend her frontal lobes (the "do it" centers) to the child. Don't worry; it's bloodless. But it's likely to be necessary for sometime. Hopefully, your child's frontal lobes will master these skills well before he gets married. We certainly hope so! If not, his secretary, wife, or girlfriend (hopefully not all at the same time) can take over your role.

Many kids know *what* to do. They just can't *do* it. That's where your supervision comes in.

How Will He Ever Learn
If We Keep Helping Him?

We know of a sixth-grade teacher who announced to a group of aghast parents on open house night, "This is a good year for your child to fail." You could hear the jaws drop. Most of the parents didn't think that *any* year was a particularly good year for their child to fail. Now, I think I know what this excellent teacher meant. His point was that most kids who are left to sink or swim will sink once and vow that it will never happen again, and that middle school is a good time for that to happen—before it shows up on their transcript for college. Indeed, most kids *do* learn by sinking or swimming when it comes to organization—except for those whose brain can't help but sink when left without a life jacket.

> Letting a child who has trouble completing a task "sink" is about as fair and helpful as letting a child who has dyslexia "sink" when she keeps reading poorly.

Our suggestion is to be the child's safety net. Monitor the child's progress while standing close by in the background. There is no harm to the child's learning curve if, for example, you double-check that she put her homework in the homework folder. And if she occasionally forgets to do the needed task, then fortunately, you are there to be her safety net and provide a softer landing for her poor executive skills. It's not fair that the child fail math, for example, simply because she is disorganized.

Be the child's safety net. Monitor the child's progress while standing close by in the background. Most of the time, you won't be needed, but there's no harm in standing by.

Safety nets are how they do it in the Olympics. The spotter steps in to monitor the athlete's dangerous maneuvers, and no one accuses the spotter of interfering with the athlete's need to take her own skills seriously. Most of the time, the spotter is not needed; but when he is needed, thankfully he is there. Be your child's safety net. Allowing severe failure does not teach skills.

Give It Time

Unfortunately, there is no exact timetable to give parents for organizing their child. In our practices, we have noticed that if a child is somewhat anxious, the anxiety may actually accelerate the organizing process. On the flip side, if a child does not appear to be anxious about his clutter or disorganization, the process may take a bit longer. Either way, the process does take time. It may go quicker if you can make organizing fun and somewhat exciting for your child. Remember, if you feel frustrated about your child's lack of organizational strategies, imagine how she feels.

If All Else Fails, Consider a Coach

If your relationship with your child is deteriorating because you love him so much that you keep trying to help him even when he can't tolerate it, then it might be time to call in a professional coach or tutor. Then you can return to your role as parent.

A coach not only teaches skills but checks in frequently to ensure that they are being carried out. Wise coaches try to establish a mutual trust with the student but still require proof that the child is actually doing what he says he is. You can find a coach through your doctor, the school psychologist, or by contacting www.edgefoundation.org, www.addcoaching.com, or www.CHADD.org.

Onward and Upward

In the next brief chapter, we'll discover how to determine your child's organizational style. Then we'll quickly put this information to work.

Chapter 2

What Is My Child's Organizational Style?

"You can imagine what my child's room looked like: clothes on the floor, dresser drawers open with clothes half hanging out of them, and toys spread all over the floor. I remember telling my daughter for the fifth time to clean it up. After the sound of her feet stomping into her room, the whole household heard, 'I need your help! I tell you all the time that I don't know how to do this! You never listen to me!' I couldn't understand this. How could a person not know how to clean up after herself? Come on! How hard could this be? Frankly, I was annoyed. Then, as I sat there on her bed, watching the tears running down her cheeks. I started to actually listen to her. She was telling me exactly what the problem was—she really didn't have a clue how to start the task. She wasn't being lazy or trying to get away from her responsibilities. She simply didn't know how to organize herself. That insight helped me to turn aside my anger. Now I just needed to figure out how to help her."

For so many children, cleaning their room, taking the empty glass of milk from the family room back to the kitchen, remembering to have the test signed, or placing school papers into the appropriate folders can be insurmountable tasks. There are so many arguments between parents and children over such organizing issues. When we experienced this as parents, we realized that something was not working. Why is organizing so complicated for some people? Do people have different styles of organization?

Why Can't My Child Use My Organizing Techniques?

Parents try their best to teach their children how to organize the way they organize. The main problem with this method? It usually doesn't work. Rather than imposing our own method, we need to learn how a given child best organizes himself. Everyone's brain organizes and recalls information differently. Let's take a further look at organizing styles.

Yes, There Is an Organizing Style

In *How to Get Organized Without Resorting to Arson*, Liz Franklin uses "access styles" to help determine organizational styles. Access styles describe how people access (i.e., retrieve) stored information and how people organize their thoughts. We have adapted this concept for children, taken how students learn into account, and incorporated those ideas into organizing styles. These styles influence how a person thinks of past events, forms habits, categorizes items, and finds those items. People utilize three basic organizing styles: visual, spatial/cozy, and chronological/sequential.

VISUAL ORGANIZERS . . .

- Think of missing items in relation to the place they last saw the item
- Need to have all their items visible
- Have a hard time finding items they cannot see
- Respond well to color, pictures, and other visual cues
- Feel disorganized when their work area is visually overloaded

SPATIAL/COZY ORGANIZERS . . .

- Think of missing items in relation to the place they last used the item
- Need to have all supplies within reach when doing schoolwork
- Need to have their work area cleaned off
- Need a work area that "feels good" to them before they can start work
- Like dance, music, and drama
- Are sensitive to how they and others are feeling
- Feel disorganized when their work area is a mess

CHRONOLOGICAL/SEQUENTIAL ORGANIZERS . . .

- Think of missing items in relation to the time they last had the item
- Access information chronologically
- Think with numbers

- Remember dates, times of events, and the order of events
- Can remember sequential steps in some sort of personal order
- Keep stacks of paper on their desks that may appear messy, but there is a certain order to the piles
- Look at detail
- Memorize best through repetition
- Feel frazzled when their work area is not in "order"

How to Find Your Child's Organizing Style

Some parents will look at the categories above and will immediately recognize their child's organizational style. If you're still not sure of your child's style, don't fret. We've developed a short questionnaire to assist you.

What's My Child's Organizing Style?

1. When your child is looking for his backpack, he asks you
   a. "Did you see my backpack?"
   b. "Do you know where I put my backpack?"
   c. "Do you know when I last had my backpack?"

2. When your child is doing her homework, she
   a. puts all the items she'll need for the homework out in front of her
   b. clears off the area before she does her homework
   c. stacks her homework assignments in a certain order before or after completing the assignments

3. Your child responds best to a teacher who
   a. writes the notes on the board
   b. makes her feel good about herself
   c. runs a very structured and orderly class

4. When your child is invited to a party, he
   a. decides how much fun he thinks the party will be based on the design of the invitation
   b. thinks about what he will do at the party
   c. wonders how long the party will be

5. You have noticed that your child likes to
   a. look at pictures
   b. build with blocks or Legos
   c. play with electronic devices

6. When your child returns from a playdate, he
   a. describes what his friend's house looked like
   b. describes how he felt at the playdate
   c. describes detailed events of the playdate in the order
      that they took place

7. Would your child rather go to a
   a. movie
   b. physical activity class such as gymnastics, dance, or
      soccer
   c. computer trade show

8. When picking out a book at the library, your child
   looks for
   a. the book with the nicest cover
   b. a title that he feels good about
   c. a book about history or a biography

If you answered mostly a, your child may be considered to have a visual organizational style. If you answered mostly b, your child may be considered to have a spatial/cozy organizational style. If you answered mostly c, your child may be considered to have a chronological/sequential organizing style.

Uh-Oh! My Child May Have Two Organizing Styles

Don't be alarmed, there's nothing wrong with your child if she has a combination of styles. A common combination style is visual-spatial. These children will like puzzles, have a great imagination, be sensitive to their feelings, and have a poor sense of time. We wouldn't be surprised if many people reading this book have children with the visual-spatial style. These are the children who are so often labeled "disorganized."

We'll use this information to help fine-tune the organizational techniques in the rest of this book.

Chapter 3

Choosing and Setting Up
the Supplies

Now that you've established your child's organizational style, let's get down to business. In this chapter, we'll discuss (1) getting the supplies, and (2) setting up the workspace.

Section I: Choosing the Supplies

Before running to the local office supply store to buy every organizing tool you can find, let's stop and look at which items will be best suited to your child's organizational style. Throughout the chapter, we will discuss items suggested in a school supply list for elementary and middle school children found on the next page.

Shopping List of Supplies

- backpack
- planner
- monthly calendar (or weekly Post-it calendar with Post-its)
- binder (three-inch if it is for all subjects, or one- or two-inch for single subjects)
- bifold folder(s) of durable plastic
- accordion file (if being used instead of the binder and folders)
- notebooks
- reinforced loose-leaf paper
- plastic binder dividers
- pencil case that fits in a binder
- pens
- pencils
- erasers
- three-hole punch that fits in a binder
- six-inch ruler
- tape
- stapler
- paper clips
- calculator
- file box
- hanging file folders
- colored file folders

○ index cards with file box for flash cards (optional)

○ clock

○ timer

○ wire mesh container to hold supplies for the transportable "office" (optional)

○ locker shelves

○ locker Book Checker

Backpacks and the Black Hole

Let's begin with the dreaded backpack. If we had a dime for every backpack we've seen that literally looked like something exploded in it, we would be sitting on some remote island for a year sipping exotic fruity drinks. Frankly, we're just thankful when nothing is growing in the backpack. But we don't need to tell you how messy they can be for disorganized children. We can tell you, though, that you need to buy a backpack that is durable, comfortable, and doesn't have a lot of pockets.

Across the board, the many pockets in the new hip backpacks usually result in lost items. At first, the visual-spatial child might love all the cool-looking pockets, thinking that they will be able to use every one of them for some trinket. These children may like the feel of the backpack and insist on buying it. Beware.

Take a look for yourself. Go get your child's current bag and look through the pockets. What do you find? Junk, candy wrappers, broken pencils, change, a missing key . . . the list goes on.

Our backpack recommendations:

- Have your child accompany you to buy the backpack. He needs to select it.
- Try to find backpacks with limited outside pockets.
- A middle school child's backpack needs to be bigger than an elementary school child's, in order to accommodate the increased number of books.

Visual organizers prefer backpacks with lots of colorful designs.

. . . .

Try to find backpacks with limited outside pockets. More pockets = more places to lose things.

. . . .

✓ VISUAL ORGANIZERS will prefer a colorful-looking backpack.

✓ SPATIAL ORGANIZERS will not only want the backpack to feel good but must be able to move their arms easily while wearing it. Also make sure that the backpack has padding in the back part of the bag for added comfort when carrying around school items with sharp edges. AirPack backpacks (www.coreproducts.com) are wonderful for kids who need extra back support in their backpacks. Their design takes the pressure off the back and distributes it between the hips. It's a great concept that is long overdue.

Spatial organizers prefer backpacks that feel good. Note the lumbar support.

Chronological organizers prefer backpacks with compartments that provide order.

✓ CHRONOLOGICAL ORGANIZERS may prefer a backpack with inside compartments to store specific materials, like the JanSport Equinox backpack, which has three compartments.

> To make sure the backpack is big enough, put all of the school supply list items inside of it. If you can close it, perfect. If not, keep shopping.

Planner

If your school does not issue homework planners, then head to the local office supply store or go online to find a planner that will meet the needs of your child. Remember, your child is using this planner, not you. You can guide your child to the type of planner for his organizing style, but you cannot force him to use the one *you* want him to use.

Some new planners are very ornate, with many different sections on a page. For example, on the bottom corner, there could be a quote of the week. Many school-issued planners also have boxes sectioned off for subjects. The planner should have easily visible lines with about ¼ inch of space between them. Make certain the subjects that are listed next to the boxes can be read clearly.

> Some students view planners as instruments of torture.

Here are some helpful hints when purchasing a planner for your child:

✓ FOR THE VISUAL CHILDREN, look for color inside, but not something so gaudy that it is distracting to the child. The more elaborate and vibrant the outside cover, the easier it will be to locate.

Planner with a week spread across two pages.

✓ **FOR THE SPATIAL AND CHRONOLOGICAL CHILDREN,**
look for planners that display the week on a two-page spread. We
happen to like this type of planner for all children. It will also help
them with time-management skills as they learn how to plan out
their week.

For some children, the planner is perceived as a way to torture
them—"Why do I need to use this again?" We can usually find an
answer to your child's concerns, so wipe the sweat off your brow.

If your child's concern is that he does not like the bulky size of
the planner, you can purchase a smaller-sized planner (similar to
the ones given out in high school). They usually have three days
listed on the left page and four days listed on the right page, with
Saturday and Sunday in much smaller boxes.

If your child uses the excuse "Well, I just lose them anyway,"
then ask her a few questions to get to the root of the problem. Is it
that she isn't organized enough to find it? Or is it that it hasn't been
working for her, so she doesn't bother keeping track of it? Ask:

- If you had to design your planner, what would it look like?
- How would the days be laid out?

- What would be the size of the planner?
- Do you like to use Post-its?

If she can answer these questions, search the office supply stores or Internet for a planner that fits her answers. Try www .successbydesign.com. We particularly like Success by Design model 2045D. If she still refuses to use a planner, there is another solution—Post-its in a wallet.

POST-ITS AND WALLET (INSTEAD OF THE PLANNER) Instead of using a planner, a child may prefer to carry in his pocket a wallet with Post-its inside. He writes each assignment on a separate Post-it, leaving them in the wallet. When he gets home, he places them on his desk or calendar. Look for Post-it wallet at www.containerstore.com.

Wallet to hold Post-its.

Monthly Calendar

Monthly calendar projects that are not due immediately need to be marked on a monthly calendar—this way the student can see visually what projects are coming up.

POST-IT CALENDAR (INSTEAD OF THE TRADITIONAL MONTHLY CALENDAR) Post-it makes a weekly calendar. It's colorful, fun, and very easy to use. There are fifty-two lined sheets in a variety of designs that cater to girls and boys. Each lined sheet is divided into eight columns, allowing the first column to be used for tasks, subjects, or other daily activities that will occur during the week. The other seven columns are for the seven days of the

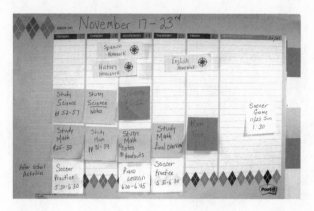

The weekly Post-it calendar.

week. Along with the sheets come a few vibrant-colored one-by-one-inch Post-its on which each task is written. You have the option of writing your individual tasks directly onto the calendar as well as using the Post-its.

Binders

Some schools require a certain color and size binder for each class. For example, we've seen many school districts that ask for a two-inch D-ring binder (where the two metal inside prongs form the letter "D"). Unfortunately, multiple binders mean multiple places to hide and lose important papers. Plus, four big binders in a backpack can be quite heavy. So, if possible, buy a *single* two- or three-inch D binder for all subjects.

If your child's school requires many individual binders and he does not want to deviate from the supply list, let him use the multiple binders for the first two weeks of school. Come to an agreement that if papers become misplaced or missing within these two weeks, he should start using a single binder. Usually children will

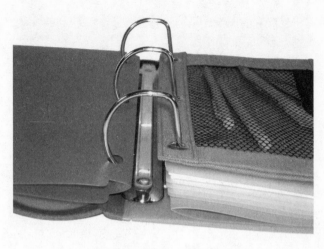

A three-inch D-ring binder.

agree to the arrangement since it gives them the chance to prove that they can function well with many binders.

. . . .

Multiple binders mean more places for important papers to hide. If your child's school does not have requirements on school supplies, buy a *single* two- or three-inch D-ring binder for all subjects.

. . . .

Many children with whom we work use a very durable, thick plastic binder with reinforced edges. Avoid the traditional binders with the softer plastic covering on what seems to be a strong cardboard.

✓ VISUAL ORGANIZERS will prefer a separate binder for each subject. This makes it easier to find items that relate to a given subject. Lots of papers and dividers in one binder would cause visual overload for this organizer.

✓ **SPATIAL ORGANIZERS** will like the single-binder system, which keeps all schoolwork in one accessible place.

✓ **CHRONOLOGICAL ORGANIZERS** will prefer placing subjects in a sequential list in a single binder.

Two-Pocket Bifold Folders

Buy durable, thick plastic two-pocket bifolders and label the left pocket Take Home and the right pocket Take to School. Use this single bifold to hold papers for all subjects. Put the two-pocket folder in the front of the binder. This is a child's version of the office in-box and out-box. Younger children can decorate the folder with pictures of home and of school. Some children benefit from writing exactly what goes into each side. Let them make the folders their own.

The **Take Home** pocket should contain school items that need to come home, such as:

- Class work handouts and notes.
- School handouts for parents.
- Tests that need signatures.
- In short, anything they touched that day.

The **Take to School** pocket should contain such items as:

- Homework that needs to be handed in.
- Signed tests that need to be returned to school.
- Notes for the teachers.

A parent should check the Take Home side of the folder each afternoon to see what needs to be filed or acted upon. At night, that

The bifold folder. One side for papers coming home;
the other for papers returning to school.

parent double-checks to make sure that all the finished homework is in the Take to School pocket. The child checks the Take to School side before he leaves school at the end of each day. If it isn't empty, he forgot to hand something in. It may be helpful to tell the teacher(s) about this new system.

Some children can use a separate bifold for each subject. Other children need to put all of their Take Home and Take to School work into a single bifold for all subjects. More information about using the bifold is coming up in chapter 4.

> Some children do better if they just place anything they touch each day into the Take Home section of a single bifold. (Explain the very simple rule: If it has the child's fingerprints on it from today, it goes into the Take Home section.)

THE ACCORDION FOLDER AS A REPLACEMENT FOR THE BINDER AND BIFOLD Some children love to have all of their important papers and handouts in one place. An accordion folder can meet the needs of these children. The folder will have about ten dividers for subjects. When the child opens the accordion folder, the subjects are all displayed at once. The first two sections in the front should be used as Take Home and Take to School sections, corresponding to the left and right sections of the bifold opposite. In the back, there might be a section for extracurricular activities.

If your child wants the accordion folder, we highly recommend one with a zipper to hold all the materials inside. Don't use an accordion folder with a string-and-knob closure or one that uses a clasp to close. The child won't bother closing such folders—and you want the folder closed! Zippers are faster and will outlive the plastic clasps and string. Children who like this type of folder seem to never go back to the binders.

✓ VISUAL ORGANIZERS may find the accordion folder overwhelming—too many pockets for too many papers.

The accordion folder with sections for Take Home, Take to School, and all class subjects.

✓ SPATIAL ORGANIZERS may not like the feel of the jagged edges of the zipper when they put their hands in the file papers.

✓ CHRONOLOGICAL ORGANIZERS will love the orderliness of the accordion folder.

Zippered Binders and Accordion Files

Many children consider binders or accordion files with a zipper along the outside a great invention for blocking their papers inside the binder so they won't lose them. If your child likes zipper binders/files we recommend purchasing the simple style that has one zipper that opens to a pocket on one side and a binder or an accordion folder on the other. Once again, too many compartments or pockets make for lost items.

✓ VISUAL ORGANIZERS will like using a zipper binder if it's kept neat. If it's messy, forget about it!

✓ SPATIAL ORGANIZERS may not like the feel of the jagged edges of the zipper.

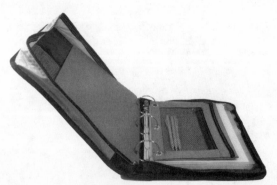

Zipper binders close with a zipper to keep all of the papers in the binder.

The Notebooks

Besides a binder, many teachers request a notebook for each subject. The variety of notebooks offered today can be overwhelming. We often hear parents say, "I stood in the supply store in front of a sea of different styles of notebooks: single-subject, three-subject, spiral, marble composition, some with folders, and some without. I couldn't decide." So let's look at each.

The classic marble notebook is virtually indestructible.

MARBLE Remember the plain black-and-white marble-design notebook with the pages stitched into the cover that us baby boomers used in school? That's the marble notebook. Teachers like these notebooks for young students because of their durability. Students cannot tear pages out of these notebooks as easily as they can from a spiral, and the hard cover makes for a longer-lasting book. Young students who are more visual may like the wider-spaced lines in these notebooks.

Wider-spaced notebook lines will give the student who struggles with penmanship a wider area to write in.

SPIRAL There are enough varieties of spiral notebooks to make your head spin. They come in single-, double-, or three-subject notebooks. The spiral notebook can be useful for students whose classes require more note-taking, especially in the middle and upper school.

Some spiral notebooks use folders inserted between the pages as subject dividers. We don't encourage actually using these folders. Rather, the two-pocket folder we've already described in the appropriate-subject binder is sufficient. Using the notebook folders can just lead to lost items. Keep it simple!

✓ **VISUAL ORGANIZERS** may find the three-subject spiral notebook overwhelming because of the multiple subjects. Use the single-subject spiral notebook.

✓ **SPATIAL ORGANIZERS** may prefer the three-subject spiral notebook because of the convenience of having a few subjects together within reach.

✓ **CHRONOLOGICAL ORGANIZERS** may like the spiral since it can fit into the binder, creating a better organizing system for them.

Pencils, Pens, Rulers, and Other Items

After you have selected a binder and placed a bifold folder in the front of it (labeled with Take Home and Take to School sections), you need to buy for the binder:

- Reinforced loose-leaf paper. This three-hole loose-leaf paper is heavier than the regular loose-leaf and also has a line of plastic from top to bottom over the holes. Ripped holes are a recipe for organizational disaster.
- Durable, thick plastic dividers with tabs to separate subjects in the binder. Do not buy paper or flimsy pliable plastic dividers. Write the subject on each divider.

The binder setup, keeping everything in one place.

- A small three-hole punch that can easily fit in the binder. Some children have complained about not having enough time to punch holes in their papers while in class. We recommend that such students place all handouts in the Take Home part of the bifold. As part of their work at home, they should hole-punch the handouts and place them in the appropriate section of the binder.
- A durable pencil case with a supply of pencils, pens, erasers, and tissues for those nasty colds. The case should have three holes so it can be inserted into a binder.
- A ruler. This can be awkward to carry. Our suggestion is to buy a six-inch ruler that fits into the pencil case.

Placing the pencil case with supplies into the three-ring binder will decrease the likelihood of your child losing materials!

The photo above shows how your child's binder should look. This strategy should satisfy all organizing styles.

The File Box and Its Folders

The binder(s) is going to fill up quickly. So where and how do you file papers that no longer need to be carried around daily? You will need to purchase the following items:

- An open, portable plastic file box with slots along the top edges to hold sliding hanging folders. You can buy these at most large office supply stores. Lightweight boxes with handles are the easiest for your child to lift. Try to buy one without a top—you want easy access for your child.
- Hanging file folders with tabs. These hanging folders have hooks at the top left and top right of the folder that slip into slots on the top edges of the file box.
- Colored file folders, two for each subject. These folders will fit inside the hanging folders.

To set up your child's filing system, first put a hanging file folder for each class into the box. Clearly write the subject on each folder's tab.

Next, ask your child to look at the colored file folders. Ask him, "What color do you see as math? Science? History?" and so on for the rest of his classes. The association of a color with a specific subject will enable him to quickly reach for the correct folder. Once he's chosen the color he'd like to use for the subject, take two folders of the same color. Label one folder Tests/Quizzes and the other Homework/Class Notes. Place the two colored folders inside that subject's hanging file in the box. Ask your child to insert the files in the order that he would like, but always keep the

The file box for tests/quizzes and homework/class notes to be saved.

two folders for each subject together in their hanging folder. We'll discuss using this simple system in chapter 4.

File Box for Flash Cards

If your child uses flash cards to study, they can be simply filed in a box as shown here.

Clocks and Timers

Many children have little or no sense of time. Several timing devices can be used to enable the student to take ownership

Flash cards can be stored in a simple file box, separated by subject dividers made out of index cards.

of the concept. Use a traditional clock with hands. Digital clocks only give numbers; they don't *show* time. (If dinner is at 5:25, and it's 4:37 now, how long do you have left to study? Quickly now!)

Don't use a digital clock! They don't give a visual sense of time.

The Time Timer gives a visual representation of the remaining time.

Find a noiseless timer that can show your child how much time is left in the study session. At www.timetimer.com, you can buy an excellent, easy-to-set, visual timer that shows a red wedge that gets smaller as the time is expiring. (We love Time Timer's desktop clocks but had some trouble figuring out how to set their wristwatches. There is also a software version for the computer.)

Wire Mesh Supply Container (Optional)

Children who need to transport their work materials—such as those who work at the kitchen table—will need a container in which to carry their supplies around. Wire mesh containers are easy to see through, which simplifies finding items.

Locker Shelves

Locker shelves will help greatly to organize the locker. They make so much sense! You can buy locker shelves by going to www.stacks andstacks.com and searching for "locker storage."

Book Checker

If you are a parent of the "Uh-oh, I left my book in my school locker" child, then you probably have created Remember to Take

Home checklists. Many parents use this list (which is placed in the locker) to help their children remember what to bring home—to avoid having to make that drive back to school for the missing book.

The Book Checker is a fantastic organizing tool for students to remind them what school items need to come home or stay at school. It is a five-by-seven-inch plastic board that is placed on the inside door of the student's locker. The board has two columns: The left column lists the student's current classes, and the right column has slots where the student can move a slide to display either Home or School. For example, if a student needs to bring home his math book, he will look at the math class listing on the left of the board and move the corresponding slide on the right to display Home.

With the Book Checker, students will become more organized at school and have all study materials with them at home when needed. Parents can also use this item at home to remind their child what items need to stay at home and/or be returned to school. You can find Book Checkers at www.thekidorganizer .com.

Section 2: Setting Up the Study Area

Okay, you've got your supplies. It's time to choose and set up the study area. A desk is the most obvious place to study, although we'll also discuss other sites, such as the kitchen table (especially for younger students), the bed, or even the bedroom floor. Let's start with the desk.

Is There a Desk Underneath That Pile of Rubble?

Matt and I met at his house. After some brief greetings with his mom, Susan, we walked up to Matt's room. I stood in the doorway, looked around quickly, and noticed that his bed was made, there was not a shirt or a sock in sight, and I could actually see his floor. I was impressed.

Susan invited me to walk farther into Matt's room. And there Susan stood, with a bright smile and her arms extended to one side—as if she were Carol Merrill from *The Price Is Right* showing a new washer and dryer—presenting "the desk." Matt's desk. It was the typical hutch on top of a desk. The top shelf had about twenty trophies, ten ribbons hanging off the sides, Happy Meal figurines, a bobblehead, souvenirs, etc. The middle shelf was filled with books and loose items. The desk—well, as my mother would say, it looked like a bomb hit it.

Matt and I removed everything and made piles on the floor: trophies/medals, DVDs/CDs, figurines, books, notebooks, pictures, and Mom's pile (a collection of items we weren't sure if Mom wanted to save). Matt was so excited that his desk was cleared. When I asked him how it felt, he responded, "Clean, a fresh start."

With the piles on the floor, Matt and I decided which items he truly needed on his desk, which would be stored in his closet in a clear plastic bin, and which would be thrown out or donated. There was some compromising going on while we went through this activity, giving Matt a sense of empowerment.

We now had a clean desk to work with. I had Matt sit in his desk chair, close his eyes, and tell me what items he used on his desk to study and do homework. After naming an item, I had Matt reach to the place on his desk he imagined the item would be. We performed this activity until all his essential items were placed. Matt chuckled and threw me a few dubious looks while participating in this activity, but ultimately he found the exercise very helpful. Matt noted that he liked an uncluttered desk where he could find things more easily. I suggested to Matt that he place the items that he might use throughout the week, such as a dictionary, textbooks, books, etc., on the second shelf. The top shelf was reserved for items that he did not need to use regularly during the week or just used sporadically. We looked back at the piles on the floor and selected only a few items from each pile to be placed on the desk.

Since Matt was interested in participating, we were able to accomplish our goal in one session. However, we did not empty the desk drawers or set up a filing system. I made another date with Matt to tackle these tasks, and they were presented separately so as not to overwhelm him. We collaborated on the amount of time we would spend on each activity before taking a break. When the timer rang after twenty minutes, Matt took a five-minute break and then returned to the desk.

Start by Cleaning Off the Desk

Clearing the desk can seem very overwhelming to a child. For the past few years, she's probably been using it for storage of her DVDs, magazines, toys, pictures, and various souvenirs. For a disorganized child, having to clear the mess off the desk is a feat of unimaginable proportions. Really.

Don't you avoid having to clean out that garage? Well, your kids are no different from you. If anything, the task may seem more anxiety provoking for children since their coping skills are not as developed as adults'. We need to assure children that they are not alone in this activity. Using the team approach—along with breaking up the task into smaller segments—will lessen your child's anxiety about starting the job.

Since many children have difficulty with the concept of time, some big tasks (like cleaning a desk) will seem like they will take weeks to accomplish. Showing your child "time" with a dial timer, like the Time Timer or those used in the kitchen, will help him have a better conceptual understanding of time. Discuss with him how much time he thinks certain tasks will take. Choose a small chore, such as making his bed or packing his school bag. Ask how much time he thinks the task will take; then time him while he completes the job. He probably overestimated the time required for the task.

Now that your child has a clearer concept of time, decide on the length of the working sessions and what section of the desk you will work on first. When you have made this decision, set the timer, start the job, and then break after your timer goes off. If your child starts to lose interest in the activity, don't yell. Show him the timer and remind him of the mutually agreed-upon time and the importance of committing to the agreement. Keep it positive, and leave a little room for negotiation.

Next, Begin to Place Study Items on the Work Area

Regardless of where your child chooses to work, have him sit at his workstation. Clear the area. Ask him to close his eyes and name an essential item he needs while studying or completing his homework. (If the child has difficulty with imagery, he can participate in this activity with his eyes open.) Have him reach for where he would imagine the item should be placed. Once he does this, have him open his eyes to see where he put his hand. Place the item at the spot he indicated. Repeat this process with all the essential items.

What are the essential items? These objects will more than likely include pens, pencils, notebooks, paper, tape, a stapler, paper clips, and a calculator. The file box will usually go on the floor if it is on wheels; otherwise, it needs to go on top of the desk. Other supplies might include a computer, printer, iPod, drink, or snack. A healthy snack fuels the brain. Hungry kids will waste time focusing on their hunger rather than their schoolwork. Besides, hunger makes people nasty and aggressive.

iPod? Yes. TV? No!

We have a number of clients who benefit from background music. It functions as white noise and may certainly be less distracting than hearing everyone else in the family mill around the house. For children who have memory issues, the white noise may actually increase their brain activity to a point where they can be more productive. Of course, we are not talking about blasting the music so loud that your neighbors down the block can hear every word of the song.

Notice that we did not endorse TV, which is much too distracting and leads to long periods of being off-task. Texting, instant messaging (IM), and video chatting also can be detrimental to studying. Yes, there may be a case where a student needs to contact a friend via IM or texting for clarification on an assignment, and this type of communication is a quick and easy way to find the solution. However, we strongly recommend that you monitor your child's use of texting and IM, especially when he is studying. Many parents have opted to put the computer that has an Internet connection in a communal area for easier parental monitoring. It's a great idea.

✓ THE VISUAL-STYLE DESK AND WORK AREA The desk of the visual-style child will have all of her essential items within her viewing range (see the photo on the next page). If an item is tucked away in a drawer, the visual child will forget about it. Avoid using drawers to store important files that your child uses weekly. Instead, use the open file box with a removable top to give the child easy viewing access. Also avoid deep containers such as ones that hold pens; you'll never see what's at the bottom of the container. If buying a new desk for your visual organizer, buy one without a lot of drawers. You may want to buy attached

The visual organizer's desk setup. Note that everything is easily visible, including the file box.

hutch shelves or install shelves yourself—it's easy to find things visually on an open shelf.

If your visual child is working in a very cluttered area, either move her to a mutually agreeable area or clean the clutter. Your child is sensitive to what she sees. If there are a lot of visual stimuli at her work area, she will be easily distracted.

Remember, "Out of sight, out of mind" is the motto for the visual-style child.

Also, you may want to take into consideration the amount of light in the work area. Some students are very sensitive to light and might work better under a dimmer light than a fluorescent one.

✓ THE SPATIAL/COZY-STYLE DESK AND WORK AREA A spatial organizer has to feel good when she sits at her desk. The imagery exercise mentioned earlier will be of particular importance to the spatial organizer. She will need to have everything on her desk within reach. Therefore, keep all essential items within an arm's length of the child. (See the photo below.)

These children need to feel good about their space. Not only will they want their study kit within reach at all times, but they will want to be able to move freely. Remember, they are the students who learn best while moving. When studying or completing homework, they may sit for ten minutes but then will need to stand up. They may also at times like to lie on the floor while studying.

If buying a new desk for the spatial organizer, you might want to consider an L-shaped desk or working table. These desks will allow your child ample space to store items that he will need on a regular basis. Spatial organizers may also like open file cabinets on wheels. These can be rolled next to the child when he's using the files and moved under the desk when not in use.

The spatial organizer's desk should keep everything within arm's reach but allow movement, as an L-shaped desk does.

Avoid buying items for the desk that have sharp or jagged edges on them; everything needs to feel comfortable. Similar to the visual organizer's needs, do not buy deep containers. They don't provide easy access to items.

✓ **THE CHRONOLOGICAL/SEQUENTIAL-STYLE DESK AND WORK AREA** The chronological-style child will set up her desk in an order that *she* finds logical (see page 54). She may place items according to the order in which she uses them. Containers that are stackable may work well for this child, since she can access material in the order that she determines. She will be able to label the trays in the order that she prefers. Maybe she wants blank loose-leaf paper at the top since she uses that the most. In the next tray, she may want to put her graph paper, since she uses it every night for math homework. We suggest using mesh trays that give her a better view of what they contain.

The chronological organizers will prefer a desk with lots of desktop space to set up their computer, clock, stackable trays, and any other items that make sense in their organizing system. An L-shaped desk or a straight desktop will work for chronological organizers.

USING THE KITCHEN/DINING ROOM TABLE AS A STUDY AREA Rather than a bedroom desk, many younger children like to work at the kitchen counter or the dining room table. Why? Because when they were elementary school students, Mom was the one who helped them to complete their homework. She kept her kids in close proximity so she could cook dinner and answer homework questions simultaneously—multitasking at its best.

Since their work area also will be used for other purposes (such as family meals), children who work in a kitchen or dining

*The chronological organizer's desk might include a laptop, clock,
and stackable trays to give a sense of order.*

room need to make their work supplies portable. Your child should
have all his essential study items (pens, paper, tape, etc.) in a mov-
able box. This container should be similar to the ones that college
students use for toiletries. This system also requires a portable filing box. Equipped with the transportable materials kit and filing
box, your child will be able to study anywhere.

USING THE BED OR FLOOR AS A STUDY AREA There are a
handful of students who like to study on their bed. Many spatial
organizers prefer this area since "feeling comfortable" is so essential to them. Bed lovers like the comfort of sitting on the bed and
spreading out school materials for easy access—features particu-

larly appealing to spatial organizers. This is fine if the bed is made. Studying in an unkempt bed will result in wasted time spent looking for pens, pencils, or books in the linens.

We have worked with a handful of very spatial children who report that they like to lie on the floor while studying. Lying on their stomach provides comfort for them. They seem to frequently switch from lying on the floor to a sitting position. Books and other school items are usually within reach for easy access. If you find your child favors this style of studying and the belongings in the room do not distract her, then it's fine. Once you find your child spending more time playing with her American Girl dolls than doing her homework, it's time to change the work area.

✓ VISUAL ORGANIZERS may find working in their bed to be too distracting, especially when there are a lot of decorations on their bed.

✓ SPATIAL ORGANIZERS will love the comfortable feel of their bed and the large area to spread out their work.

✓ CHRONOLOGICAL ORGANIZERS just want to be in a workspace that contains their electronic devices.

Setting Up the Locker—the Other Black Hole

"One day, I brought my son back to school because he forgot his textbook. I decided to walk him to his locker. He opened the locker and kaboom! I stood there, jaw dropping and all, in disbelief as to what I saw—books all thrown in the locker, loose papers sticking out between the books, an old lunch, a sweatshirt I'd been *looking for, and just plain old garbage! No wonder this kid can't find anything."*

Chances are, if your child is messy at home, his locker is probably a disaster area as well. In the later years of elementary school and middle school, students may change rooms for different subjects, which may require them to go to their lockers to switch books. Teachers may check younger students' desks, but for older kids, the locker is uncharted territory, never viewed by adult eyes.

Most children's lockers represent areas of uncharted wilderness never exposed to adult eyes.

LOCATION, LOCATION, LOCATION (EVEN FOR LOCK-ERS) Try to get a locker at the end of the row, which allows for more elbow room. Opt for a locker that is at eye level so that the child doesn't have to crouch down to look into it. Also, if a child has a lower locker and has knelt down to switch books, he is at ear level with the slamming locker doors. For a child who is sensitive to sound, this clanking can be a distraction.

✓ VISUAL ORGANIZERS may find that a locker at the end of the row offers fewer visual distractions.

✓ SPATIAL ORGANIZERS may like to have a locker at the end of a row for more elbow room.

✓ CHRONOLOGICAL ORGANIZERS may want a locker located close to their classes to minimize the time needed to move between them.

WHAT SHOULD BE IN THE LOCKER? If you walk into any office supply or large chain store starting late July through September, you can't help but look at all the school supplies. In recent years, we're sure you've noticed a surge in locker decorations: mirrors, organizers, plastic holders, whiteboards, etc.

Some students have a white dry-erase board hanging, but after some time, the novelty wears off. The marker is gone, they're in too much of a rush to stop and jot down a note to themselves, or, after a while, they don't even notice the board anymore.

We've seen many parents make lists of reminders for their forgetful children. These lists are very helpful if the student utilizes them. The Book Checker is a practical tool that kids can use to remember the books they need to bring home. Place the Book Checker on the inside of the locker door.

Some children use locker shelves to divide the locker. This allows the student to maximize locker space. He can store books on two levels, putting the books for the morning classes on the top level and those for the afternoon classes on the bottom.

Locker shelves will help prevent a massive pileup of materials.

Students should keep in their locker a supply of pencils, pens, erasers, Post-its, tissues, and small plastic grocery bags. Plastic bags? Yes, you can always use an extra bag for emergencies.

If your children have to change their wardrobe for physical education, try to send them to school with an extra pair of sneakers and a change of clothes. You can put the extra set of clothes in a large Ziploc bag. They'll stay together at all times.

LOCKERS FOR DIFFERENT ORGANIZATIONAL STYLES

✓ VISUAL ORGANIZERS need to see items directly; otherwise, they will have a difficult time finding the items. This is no small feat since lockers are usually narrow and deep. Parents of visual children have probably heard their child say on many occasions, "Last time I saw it, it was in my locker. Now I have no idea where it is." Chances are that the item is still in the locker, but in the back, out of sight of the student. Remind your child to keep everything up toward the locker door and not in the back. If she came home claiming to have lost a school paper, ask her to look in the back of her locker. You never know, it just might be sitting there, waiting patiently to be discovered. Locker shelves might work particularly well for the visual student.

✓ SPATIAL ORGANIZERS will need to have all of their locker items in the locker within their reach. Similar to visual children who cannot find an item without seeing it, spatial children will have difficulty finding an item that is not within their reach.

✓ CHRONOLOGICAL ORGANIZERS will want the locker to have some sort of order to it. The placement of books and other items will make sense to them, and maybe only them. Items will be stacked according to their method. They may want to use the locker shelves or may opt out. As long as their piles of books, notebooks, and binders remain in order, they will feel organized.

Summary

....

When buying supplies, try to take into account your child's organizational style. See pages 27–28 for a list all of the supplies needed by most students. In particular, your child will need:

- A backpack that has few outside pockets (which are mini black holes). Test whether it is large enough to hold all of the supplies.
- A planner or Post-it wallet to record assignments.
- A monthly calendar (or weekly Post-it calendar).
- A bifold folder.
  - The left, Take Home side is where the child places any papers he touched that day. When he comes home, this side is the only place he needs to look for the day's materials.
  - The right, Take to School side is where all papers go that are being handed in tomorrow. When the student is asked for his homework, there is only one place it can be—and a parent double-checked that it was there the night before.
- A single two- or three-inch binder for all subjects, if allowed by the school. A single binder means fewer places for papers to hide.
- Dividers for the different subjects within the binder.
- As an alternative to the binder and dividers, an accordion file for all subjects. If the child uses an accordion file, the first two sections can function as the Take Home and Take to School folders.

- A binder or accordion file that can be zippered, if it suits the student's organizational style.
- A pencil case that fits into the binder (so the student can't lose it).
- Pencils, pens, erasers, a six-inch ruler, and tissues for the pencil case.
- Reinforced loose-leaf paper.
- Notebooks: marble or spiral.
- A file-box system to keep the binder(s) from filling up quickly.
  - An open, portable plastic file box with slots along the top edges to hold sliding hanging folders.
  - Hanging file folders with tabs for each subject.
  - Colored file folders, two for each hanging folder. Label one folder Tests/Quizzes and the other Homework/Class Notes.
- Locker supplies, especially locker shelves and the Book Checker.

Set up the child's work area according to his organizational style.

- Younger children often like to work in the kitchen. They will need a wire mesh basket to create a portable office.
- Most kids will work at a desk, although some will prefer the bed or the floor.
- Keep electronic distractions to a minimum, although generally iPods are okay and may even be beneficial.
- Snacks keep students happy.

Chapter 4

Follow the Paper Trail: Getting Work Home, Doing It, and Returning It

Congratulations! Your child now has the correct supplies and an appropriate place to use them. The basics are all in place. All that's left is to do the work! That involves following the paper trail.

The paper trail:

- starts with getting the *correct* assignments and materials home,
- continues with the child planning and doing the work, and
- ends with the work being returned to school or filed.

Let's work out techniques for each of these steps. You might want to take a minute to look at the summary on pages 91–93 at the end of this chapter, if you haven't already done so. (The technique of reading the summary before reading the actual chapter is coming up in the *next* chapter—so we forgive you if you haven't done it yet.)

Getting Assignments from School to Home—Ugh!

One of the biggest complaints from the parents of disorganized children concerns missing papers that never seem to safely make it back and forth between school and home. These papers could be assignments, homework sheets, tests/quizzes, information from the school, or permission slips. Something always seems to happen to these papers when they have to travel from school to home or vice versa.

Where *do* all of those papers go that never seem to make it safely from school to home and back? Some sort of paper heaven, we suppose.

We're sure you've probably tried a number of different techniques to secure papers in their travels. If you're reading this section, your techniques probably didn't work. Let's explore some of the strategies that have worked for our clients. Remain cognizant of your child's organizational style in order to develop and tweak a successful plan.

Getting the (Correct) Assignments and Work Home

1. The child records the assignments by using a:
   - planner,
   - Post-it wallet, or
   - electronic program.

2. Make sure the assignments are correct by setting up a safety net utilizing a:
   - classroom buddy or a teacher to check the assignment pad, and/or
   - class web page, and/or
   - emergency call from home to a peer to fill in missing assignments.

3. Get the correct handouts/papers home by using the bifold folder.

Recording Assignments with a Planner

"I hate using planners; they never work for me! I just remember all my assignments in my head." ("True," you think, "except for the assignments he forgets.")

"I don't need a planner. All I have to do is look at the website for the homework."

"I used the planner in September, and by October the cover was completely off. I'm not sure exactly where it is these days."

These are all actual statements from some of the children we've worked with. We have found that most children will use some sort of planner—at least sporadically—but there is a small group of children who refuse to use one at all. After all, writing assignments down in a planner is not an easy task for most disorganized children.

Your mission, should you decide to accept it, is to direct the child to the point where he acknowledges the importance of some sort of an assignment book. Some children catch on to the technique of using a planner. Then there are others who just never seem to get it. They might benefit from using a Post-it wallet.

Putting a paper clip on the current page of the planner will make finding today's information easier.

Tommy's Post-it Wallet

Tommy was an eighth-grader who hated any type of planner. He prided himself on his good memory and relied on it to remember the homework and projects due during the week. However (you knew there was going to be a "however"), Tommy forgot to complete some assignments and projects because he didn't write down the information.

We asked Tommy to do the following math problem:

Imagine that you did four homework assignments and got a score of 90 on each of them. Then you forgot about the fifth and got a 0 on it. What's your new average?

90

90

90

90

0

New average: 72

Tommy admitted that he probably would have received better grades if he had handed all the work in on time. So he did realize the importance of a planner. Then our mission was to find one that worked for him.

Tommy was a visual-spatial child. He loved color and the feel of many different objects, such as fuzzy stuffed animals. There was another item Tommy liked—Post-its.

When Tommy and his mom went shopping, they found a wallet for Post-its. The greatest thing about the wallet was that it could fit in his pocket because it was not too bulky. Tommy loved the idea of using the Post-it wallet but especially liked that he could carry it in his pants pocket.

We discussed how to use the wallet. When an assignment was given, Tommy would take out his wallet and write the assignment on a Post-it, leaving it attached to the pad. For the next class, he flipped to the second Post-it and wrote the new assignment. Tommy continued to do this for all his classes, never taking the Post-its off until he arrived home at his desk. When he sat down to begin his work, Tommy would remove the Post-its from his wallet and stick each one in eyeshot on his desk. As he completed an assignment, he threw out the Post-it.

At our next visit, Tommy was excited to show me how he used the Post-its. He felt that the technique was unique and quite fun. In fact, some of his friends were going to try this strategy instead of using a planner!

Recording Assignments in a Post-it Note Wallet

We have worked with older children who love using Post-its inside a wallet. (Younger students may not have pockets large enough to fit the wallet.) Children love the fact that they can carry the wallet around in their pocket from class to class, making it simultaneously more convenient and harder to lose. Students also like that they can peel the Post-its off when they get home and use them as homework reminders. As we'll see, this system can be adapted to both short- and long-term projects.

Recording Assignments Electronically

Computer-savvy children who can arrange access to a computer at school may wish to record their homework electronically by creating an Excel or Word document, with a shortcut to the document placed on the computer's desktop for easy retrieval. If your child opts for this technique, her assignments will be saved in the program for her to print at home. She can use her printout as a checklist for completing her homework. Kids may be intrigued by the programs, which employ innovative means to record assignments.

Your child might find helpful the Digital Notes software on the Post-it website at www.postit.com. (Search the site for "Digital Notes.") You can download the program for a free thirty-day trial period to see if your child likes it. The program has the same concept as paper Post-its, but your child will be posting electronic Post-its on his desktop. StudyMinder, at www.studyminder.com, also has a simple homework organizer that keeps track of work times. StudyMinder also has a free trial download.

✓ CHRONOLOGICAL ORGANIZERS may be attracted to these electronic strategies since they involve technology.

Making Sure the Assignments Are Correct

Using one of the techniques above, your child has done his best to record his assignments. How do we make sure that they're correct?

Checking Assignments via Direct Communication with the Teacher

"Brendan's teacher is great. She initials his agenda book and will contact me if he misses homework or forgets to hand something in. She's my eyes and ears at school."

In the later years of elementary school and into middle school, students usually start to move from class to class. They have many responsibilities, including getting to class on time, bringing the right books to class, and juggling multiple teachers and their assignments. For the disorganized child, this can be an absolute nightmare!

Coping with multiple teachers during middle school can be an organizational nightmare!

We promote proactively enlisting the aid of your child's teacher(s). If your child has some learning or other issues that might impede his success, we recommend contacting the teacher and guidance counselor before school starts in September. Write an e-mail introducing yourself, explaining your concerns, and giving your contact information. Making this contact during the summer, when your child's teachers are not in the midst of a hectic school day, will allow the teachers to focus more on your concerns. If you need feedback from many teachers, contact your child's guidance counselor (who can gather the information) or ask for a team meeting.

Don't keep teachers in the dark about your Joey's forgetfulness and disorganization. Who else will be your helper at school? Who will immediately inform you that Joey forgot to hand in his homework? Who will let you know if he is forgetting to bring his sneakers to gym? Who will tell you if his grades are affected by his disorganization? How will the teacher know that such feedback is welcome? When speaking to teachers, keep it friendly. Remember, you are all on the same team—your child's!

If we don't notify a teacher about a child's problems, how will she know that it would help if she signed his planner? How will she know that his incomplete work is due to a problem with organization rather than a problem with caring?

Checking Assignments with the Buddy System

Many lower-grade elementary school classes use the buddy system. The "buddies" are children in the class who are paired, usually sitting in close proximity to each other. Before the end of the day, the teacher will make an announcement for the buddies to check each other's assignment pads to see if all assignments have been written correctly in the agenda. The teacher should be aware of the organizational skills of the children in her class and should know who would make a good and supportive pair.

Checking Assignments with an Adult at School

If the teacher states that he doesn't think he would have time to check the planner, brainstorm with the teacher (you're on the same team!) as to who would be the next choice to help your child. If your child is classified as having learning or attention issues, then asking the learning specialist may be the way to go. Otherwise, the adult could be a teacher, a guidance counselor, or an aide at the school. They can check in with the student to ensure that he has the correct assignments and materials and that he has completed his tasks. The parents could take over this job at home. The child's tasks would consist of writing homework down in the planner, packing the homework books for the night in his backpack, doing the work, and handing in an assignment to a specific teacher.

Some middle school staff feel that children of that age should start to be independent and do not want to offer "crutches."

However, you've already tried leaving your child to his own devices a few dozen times and know that doesn't work. Everyone needs to lend a helping hand, especially in the beginning.

When it comes to organization, "sink or swim" doesn't work if you can't swim yet. As your child improves with his organization, the school staff can slowly retreat and begin to function more as a safety net.

Checking Assignments via School Websites

Ah, the school website. It seems as though every school has one these days. Many teachers have their own class web pages, where they list the work for the week, homework, and upcoming tests—except when they don't. In general, though, this is a fantastic way to stay informed about the required work for each class.

The school website offers a lot of other important information, such as contact numbers and e-mail addresses of faculty and staff members. Any half days or days off should be posted on the site as well. It has been our experience that school websites link to additional websites with resources for study skills. Take the time to review your school site and utilize these resources.

Checking Assignments with the "I'd Like to Call a Friend" Lifeline

Despite all of the above, you still may find a big, fat blank space in the planner next to math or some other subject. It's hard to believe, but you still don't know whether there really isn't any math homework or your child just forgot to write it in the space. We suggest the following deal: If there really is no homework in a given subject, then the child must write out the words "No homework." If he does that, we'll believe him; after all, the child is disorganized, not dishonest. However, if there is just a blank, then the child *must* check the website or call a friend to confirm whether there was homework or not. Don't get angry. Just matter-of-factly hand him the phone and the phone number of a friend (get those in advance). Listen while he checks. Be sure to have more than one friend lined up from each class in case one of them is not home.

> If there really is no homework in a given subject, then the child must write out the words "No homework." A blank space in the planner = phone a friend.

Getting Materials Home with the Two-Pocket Folder

So, your child has the assignments, and we're pretty sure they are correct. Finally. How do we make sure that she has all of the needed papers to do the assignments—and that everyone can find them?

That's the role of the thick plastic two-pocket folders you bought (marked Take Home on one side and Take to School on the other). The real beauty of this system is that both your child and you have only one place to look for today's papers—in the Take Home section. That sure beats looking through (and between) multiple binders and folders.

> There is only one place to look for today's papers—in the Take Home section of the bifold.

At home, allow your child the opportunity to place the Take Home papers into their correct place:

- Current notes go into the proper binder section. (Some of the papers may need to have holes punched.)
- Tests/quizzes coming home go into the filing box.
- Homework to be done goes onto the work area of the desk near the planner.
- Things to be signed go to a parent.

In the beginning, you may need to guide and/or watch your child while he performs these steps. Don't expect perfect use of the bifold to happen overnight. After a while, the child will hopefully be able to do this on his own—but don't forget to be the safety net and double-check. No news from your child or his teacher is not necessarily good news!

The other side of the bifold is for handing completed work back in. More about that later—after we've discussed planning and doing the work.

Planning the Work

So, you and your child actually know what new assignments were given today. That is the role of the planner, Post-it wallet, or electronic document. Although a planner tells you what was *assigned* today, it doesn't tell you what you actually need *to do* today. After all, some of the assignments your child learned about today are not due tomorrow, and some of what he needs to do today was assigned two weeks ago. How do you keep track of all that? A planning calendar is used to map out when you are going to actually do things.

Why Do Kids Have Such a Hard Time Planning?

Jill is given an assignment on Monday that is due on Friday. The problem is that despite repeated nagging, she won't start it until Thursday night. This situation inevitably results in increased anxiety and tension. Mom is yelling at Jill, and Jill is trying to explain that she thought that she had enough time to finish the work.

Too many children suffer from the old "I'll get to it later." Come to think of it, there are many adults who suffer from this as well. (Maybe your spouse?) The ability to set long-term goals and break them down into short-term goals can be challenging for some children. There are several reasons:

- Their poor concept of time means that they really did think there was enough time.
- Their lack of foresight prevents them from recognizing the disadvantages of delaying the project.
- Their lack of hindsight prevents them from recognizing that procrastination didn't work last time.
- Children who are disorganized tend to have an extremely difficult time with initiating and executing a task all the way to completion.
- They can't resist the temptation to do something else more appealing.
- Some kids are overwhelmed by having to do a project at all, so they end up putting it off.
- Sometimes the child just forgets about the project.

Remember, most of these problems are the fault of the undeveloped brain, not the child.

Parents seem to have tried many tactics in the attempt to fight their children's "procrastination." Yelling doesn't work. (It hasn't yet, has it?) It's really not surprising since punishment does not alter a child's brain or teach the needed skills. You wouldn't expect screaming to cure dyslexia. Why should you expect it to cure a planning/organizational problem? Let's see if we can find some solutions that do work to teach your child how to plan. Planning skills will allow him to feel more confident and less stressed, and to have a sense of pride in his work.

....

In what way does punishment teach the needed skills? You wouldn't expect screaming to cure dyslexia. Why should you expect it to cure a planning/organizational problem?

....

To get your child to realize the importance of good planning, ask her the following questions. Don't forget to truly listen to her answers—the key to a solution lies in her words.

- How do you feel when your teacher assigns a project that is due next week? Does it make you feel anxious, overwhelmed, scared, bored, etc.?
- How do you start a project?
- Why do you start it later rather than today?
- When you do start the project at the last minute, do you think it affects your grade?
- How would you feel if you finished the project ahead of time? Relieved?

After your discussion, explain to your child that you can help her reduce her frustration and feel better about the project. Once again, you will work as a team to maintain a planning calendar, with specific goals to meet from now until the project is due. You will continue to guide her as needed. Simply telling the child once or twice how to do something is often not enough for them to apply the skill. Taking the time to teach *and guide* your child through these skills will result in a happier house!

The Different Types of Planning Calendars

Let's discuss using the different types of planning calendars: the planner, the monthly calendar, the Post-it calendar, and the software calendar.

USING THE PLANNER AS A PLANNING CALENDAR The planner can also function as a planning calendar. Each day, the child (perhaps with an adult providing a safety net by double-checking):

- Puts a mark next to the work in the planner that needs to be done today.
- For longer-term projects (that were assigned today but don't need to be done today), flips to the page of the planner corresponding to the due date and makes an entry, such as "English paper on WW1 due." Then the child can plan backward (or forward, if that works better for your child) to enter the dates of partial deadlines for that project. For example, three days before the due date, enter "Edit rough draft"; five days before the due date, enter "Finish rough draft"; ten days before the due date, enter "Finish reading," etc.
- Enters upcoming test dates and regularly occurring dates, such as spelling quizzes every Friday.

- Records after-school activities as well.
- Every day, your child (and an adult, if needed) not only looks at the day's entries, but flips through the next few weeks to see what's coming up, checking to see if something needs to be done today for those longer-term projects.

. . . .

Each day, your child looks at the current page of his planner as well as his monthly calendar.

. . . .

USING A TRADITIONAL MONTHLY CALENDAR AS A PLANNING CALENDAR Instead of entering upcoming dates into the appropriate page of the planner, many students prefer to write them onto a monthly calendar, which has the huge advantage of displaying everything at once (in an organized fashion). It's much easier to see projects clumping together, such as a major book report due one day before a big test. Many planners have monthly calendars in them, although they may be rather small. Some students prefer a separate monthly calendar that can be purchased from your office supply store. Don't forget to enter the partial project deadlines into the monthly calendar. Each day, the student figures out what she has to do by looking at the planner *and* at the monthly calendar.

✓ VISUAL ORGANIZERS will like to "see" the activities for the month.

✓ SPATIAL ORGANIZERS may like the spaces provided to write their activities for each date.

✓ CHRONOLOGICAL ORGANIZERS are number people— they want to know how many days are left to complete a project.

Brian and the Post-it Weekly Calendar

Brian needed to develop a time-management calendar. Since Brian was visual and chronological, we suggested that his family buy the Post-it weekly calendar. This calendar would appeal to his visual side, by allowing him to see time, and his chronological side, by establishing a system that allowed him to place the Post-its in order. Brian chose a different-colored Post-it to correspond to each category:

- homework
- actual day of a test/quiz
- study times for a test/quiz
- after-school activities

We started with after-school activities, since they usually have a set day and time each week. (Brian chose blue for that category since blue was calming to him.) Then we discussed any tests/quizzes for the week. (He chose yellow for tests/ quizzes, since yellow reminded him of an emergency.) If he had an important test on Friday, we would place a yellow "test/quiz" Post-it on Friday and work backward to place "study" Post-its on the previous days. Next, we placed the homework Post-its in the appropriate spots. A great advantage of using Post-its on this calendar is that Brian was able to move the Post-its from one slot to another if we felt that one day was overloaded with tasks. A more traditional calendar would only allow you to erase or cross out, making for a visual overload of markings. His mom was a terrific coach in our absence. She sat with Brian at the beginning of the week to help plan out the week and set aside chunks of study time.

By planning tasks for the week, scheduling times to study, and discarding Post-its when the task was complete, Brian started to feel less anxious about school and improved his grades. He was able to utilize the calendar as a true visual representation of actual time, which nurtured his visual/chronological style. He found a sense of accomplishment every time he removed a Post-it. Brian was also successful at purging his binders weekly and allowing himself to have "Brian time." More control. Less anxiety. Better results.

USING A POST-IT CALENDAR AS A PLANNING CALENDAR

We are huge fans of the Post-it calendar.

Sit with your child and explain the concept of this calendar. He has the choice to write down his class subjects or weekly activities on the far left column or just use the Post-its in the daily columns to indicate subjects. Then he needs to date the seven days of the week across the top of the next seven columns. If there is a long-term project, you should date the next page as well and place a Post-it on the due date of the project. Look again at the Post-it calendar on page 33.

One of the greatest aspects of this calendar is that your child can write the task on a Post-it, and when he has completed the task, he can throw the Post-it away. No more crossing out or creating holes in the paper from pressing on the pen too hard. The gradual unveiling of a clean calendar as the week transpires is quite visually pleasing. (Some children, though, like to write some assignments directly on the calendar.)

✓ ALL ORGANIZERS could benefit from this calendar. Children are often very excited about using it. We suggest that it be placed at eye level at the location where the child studies. The sheets are attached together to allow you to tear one off at a time in typical Post-it fashion. If your child works at the dining room table, you might want to keep each sheet attached to the pad since there might be some constraints on a hanging place.

Using the Post-it Calendar in a Nutshell

1. Write all scheduled weekly events at the bottom of each daily column (dance, music lessons, basketball practice, etc.).
2. Place Post-its for projects and tests/quizzes for the week.
3. Place Post-its for homework. We like to use the small narrow Post-its (they look like return address labels) to write down homework.
4. Make sure to use a different color or style of Post-it for each category of activity, such as study homework, projects, tests/quizzes, or after school.

5. When you complete the activity, take the Post-it off the calendar and throw it away. The spatial organizers will love the feeling of accomplishment they get by tossing the Post-it in the garbage.

6. There is no need to cross out. Just move the Post-it around to accommodate last-minute changes to the schedule.

USING A SOFTWARE CALENDAR AS A PLANNER Some children are quite computer-savvy. Okay, let's rephrase that—most children are computer-savvy. Some websites offer assorted calendars for download or online use (see appendix B). Some of these calendars are free. However, one must be thirteen years of age to use them, according to the Children's Online Privacy Act of 1998. Google offers such a calendar at www.google.com/calendar. This site allows the user to invite other individuals, such as parents, to view the calendar as well. Google Calendar can also send text-message reminders to your child's cell phone. Naturally, we are not recommending these web calendars for younger children but for older middle and high school children who have permission from their parents.

✓ CHRONOLOGICAL ORGANIZERS will love a tech calendar!

Using the Planner for Short-Term Assignments

As parents of tweens and teens, we are acutely aware of how schedules can change daily. Never mind the last-minute basketball practice, but what about Thursday's test that was just announced on Monday? Ugh! Tasks that are due within five days are typically considered short-term assignments.

If your child comes home on Monday and tells you that he has a math test on Thursday, you need to set up a schedule to study for the test. Children who feel overwhelmed by the amount of work they have to complete may need a calendar that will indicate how much time can be spent on each assignment. You may use a roomy preprinted calendar or make up your own grid on a separate piece of paper. (See the table on page 82 for an example.) Some of you are saying, "My kid would never stick to a schedule like this; it's too restrictive." You're right. Some kids may only need to put their assignments on the calendar and finish the tasks at their own pace.

When creating a schedule for the week, take into consideration the usual homework that is given nightly. Also, you need to factor in eating and bathing. Before setting up the calendar, time your child in certain activities to get a decent estimate of time needed. It is better to allot extra time in your predictions of how long a task will take rather than cut yourself short. If an assignment usually takes twenty minutes, plan for thirty minutes. If your child finishes her task ten minutes early, she can then begin her other assignments and hopefully complete those early as well.

A sample short-term study calendar. (HW="homework.")

TIME	MONDAY	TUESDAY	WEDNESDAY	THURSDAY
Projects/Test due dates			*History quiz today*	*Math test today English essay due today*
4:00–4:30	History HW	Bio HW	Bio HW	
4:30–5:00	English essay	English essay	Soccer	
5:00–5:30	Eat	Eat	Soccer	
5:30–6:00	Piano	HW	Eat	
6:00–6:30	Piano	HW	Study math	
6:30–7:00	Math HW	HW	Study math	
7:00–7:30	Study math	Study math	History HW	
7:30–8:00	Study history	Study history	English HW	

Let's set up the calendar. On Monday, Tommy was informed that he has a history quiz on Wednesday and a math test and English essay due on Thursday. He writes these project/test due dates along the top of the schedule. He needs to divide his time during the week to fit in his studying, regular homework assignments, and some after-school activities. Since Tommy has piano lessons on Monday and soccer practice on Wednesday, he wrote these two activities down in the appropriate time slots. Then he charted when he would complete his other responsibilities, including eating dinner. He could work for twenty to twenty-five minutes at a time with a five-to-ten-minute break. Tommy might choose to work past the twenty minutes and move his break back. This schedule will allow Tommy the opportunity to flip tasks to different time slots as he wishes. For example, he may decide to complete Monday's math homework when he comes home at 4:00 instead of at 6:30.

Break larger tasks into chunks and mark them on a calendar.

For the anxious child, breaking down the time into smaller increments allows him to see that he can actually finish his tasks in sufficient time. It's not as overwhelming when you "chunk" the time.

"Chunk It" to Make Work Less Intimidating

"Mom, there's no way that I can finish my essay and work on my project tonight after my volleyball game. It's too much!"

Children can feel anxious about a busy schedule. How *do* they fit basketball practice, homework, and study time for a quiz all into one day? Some days your child will be given last-minute assignments or quizzes that will overwhelm her at first. Heck, we would all feel overwhelmed by it. Remember how you feel when your boss gives you three projects all at the same time. Our experience has been that some of these overwhelmed children become victims of avoidant behavior. They're avoiding the task because it's too much work and, quite frankly, they don't know *how* to start.

When your child is inundated with homework, take a moment to help her chunk her time. Let's say Carly's biology teacher told the class today that there would be a quiz on chapter 9. Carly comes home in a panic. All she focuses on is chapter 9 as a whole.

Carly's mom listens as her child rants about not having enough time. Mom knows that she can't just ignore Carly's feelings. Helpful or not, her feelings exist and have to be dealt with. Mom, who's read this book, knows how to help Carly chunk her time into small sections so that the tasks are not as overwhelming. Mom starts by having Carly take out all of her study material for the test, so they can get a better idea of how much work needs to be studied. There happen to be twelve pages in chapter 9. Mom asks Carly to divide the chapter into three parts.

They agree on twenty-minute intervals of studying followed by five-minute breaks (to get up, stretch, get a drink, or walk around). Carly studies her English vocabulary for twenty minutes, takes a break, and then does her math. Time for dinner. Then she chunks the twelve pages of chapter 9 into three sessions of four pages each, with a five-minute break

Chunking material for a biology test.

TIME	TASKS
4:00–4:20	English vocabulary words
4:25–4:45	Math homework
4:45–5:30	Dinner
5:30–5:50	Bio pp. 1–4
5:55–6:15	Bio pp. 5–8
6:20–6:40	Bio pp. 9–12
6:45–7:05	Review bio material

between sessions. Then there is time for a review of chapter 9 (see table above).

When Mom helped Carly write down the pages she was going to work on during the twenty-minute intervals, suddenly Carly felt more confident that she would be able to accomplish her work. Obviously, it would be fine if Carly wanted to continue reading without taking a break. Chunking, or breaking up the assignments, allowed Carly to see the assignment in smaller pieces that were easier to absorb than viewing the studying as a whole. Eating a pie in small pieces is easier and less intimidating than eating the whole pie in one sitting.

Using the Planner for Long-Term Projects

When an elementary or middle school teacher gives an assign-ment that is due more than a week away, we consider this a long-term project. For such projects, teachers are giving the students enough time to complete a well-thought-out assignment. Yet so many students don't understand that teachers expect more out of long-term assignments then they do out of short-term ones. If he doesn't believe you, have your child ask the teacher why she gave the class two weeks to complete the assignment.

Sometimes, you'll just have to say no to the extra play-date, after-school activity, or music lesson. Your child may not have the maturity to know when her schedule is over-loaded.

Let's work on creating a plan to tackle a long-term project, us-ing as an example a project about a person in your child's life who has had a significant impact on him. It is due in two weeks, on October 28. The project needs to be on a poster board with pic-tures and drawings of the person along with a two-paragraph es-say. Sound typical? Let's choose Grandpa as the subject.

To set it up in the calendar, move to October 28, the due date for the project. Put on a Post-it or write directly on the calendar that the project is due on this date. What step would come right before you handed in the project? That step would be a review of your work. Put another Post-it on the twenty-sixth, marked "Review poster." That gives your child at least two days to make any last-minute changes.

Here are all the tasks in chronological order, working back-ward from the due date:

1. Hand in the project.
2. Review for mistakes or any additions.
3. Glue on the pictures and drawings.
4. Complete your written work.
5. Collect the pictures and draw some pictures of Grandpa.
6. Write a second draft of your written work.
7. Brainstorm about how you want to design the project. Discuss with someone else.
8. Speak to parents about where the pictures are. Ask them to buy poster board.
9. Write first draft of essay with the information that Grandpa gave you.
10. Interview Grandpa.
11. Ask Grandpa to be part of the project.
12. Select a person in your life.

Your child will be less overwhelmed, and more willing to start the project, once he sees that it is merely a series of simple steps.

How Long Should a Child Study Between Breaks?

Parents often ask us about when and how many breaks their children should take. Our children would bargain for breaks that were usually unreasonable and long—"I'll go back to my math homework as soon as *Hannah Montana* is over; there's only five more minutes left." How many times have you heard that? Five minutes turns into ten. Then when you threaten to turn the television off, your daughter panics and swears that she's never seen this episode and it won't ever be on again! They talk a good story, but the reality is that they need to get back to the task at hand.

What is a reasonable time to work and a reasonable time for breaks? As mentioned earlier, children like to feel empowered. Negotiating a realistic break time with your child gives him a sense of responsibility in the decision-making process. The table below gives some working guidelines.

Typical minutes for study sessions and breaks.

TYPE OF STUDENT	MINUTES PER WORK SESSION	MINUTES PER BREAK
Elementary school	15	3–5
Elementary school with attention/learning issues	10	3–5
Middle school	20–30	3–5 (A *few* more minutes if needed)

When negotiating with children, don't ignore the fact that they will be looking for something in return for following the rules, such as extra time for video games. Remember that positive reward systems only work if the child can actually get the reward—otherwise, there is nothing but frustration on everyone's part.

Returning the Work to Its Proper Place: the School or the File Box

The homework is done, but there's still one very crucial step left: getting it back to its proper destination. Basically, papers need to be either handed in or filed. Amazingly enough, this is a *major* problem for many kids.

Handing in Completed Work

"Kathy's biggest problem is that she works hard on her homework and then forgets to hand it in at school the next day. She loses five points for every homework assignment that is not submitted. I don't understand why she does this."

This is a very typical scenario for disorganized children. They complete their homework, close the books, and walk away—only to find out the next day at school that their homework is missing. How could this happen? It occurs more often than we could have imagined. Students who don't have a routine to deal with completed homework will find themselves missing homework, signed tests, etc.

When your child has completed his assignment, the paper needs to go into the two-pocket folder we have already discussed, placing it on the right, Take to School, side of the folder. This folder is taken to each and every class—no questions asked! When the teacher asks for the paper, there's only one place to look. And you know it's there because you were a good safety net and double-checked it the night before.

When the teacher asks for the paper, there's only one place to look—in the Take to School side of the bifold folder. And you know it's there because you checked!

This is a great system, if your child uses it. What happens when you try this for a couple of weeks and papers are still missing from the folder? Brainstorm with your child to find out what may have gone wrong. We have found that by listening to a child's answers to specific questions, we usually can figure out the problem.

Here are questions you may want to ask your child if the two-pocket folder is not working:

- How did you feel about using the folder?
- What didn't you like about the folder?
- Was it difficult to remember to put your papers in it?
- Was it difficult to put papers in and take them out?
- Where did you put the folder while in school?
- How many times did you take out the folder?

The answers to these questions will lead you to why the technique is not successful. Maybe Tommy doesn't really like the actual folder. Tommy may not be keeping the folder in a place where he can see it or have easy access to it. Tommy's teacher could also be handing out important papers at the end of the day, when Tommy may be focusing more on getting his backpack ready to go home. It's hard to come up with an answer without asking questions. The more you ask, the more information you will get. Listen to the answers, and be patient.

Filing Completed Work

Each day, go through the Take Home side of the bifold and put the papers into the correct place: today's work pile, the proper section of the binder, or the file box for completed tests and homework that no longer need to be carried daily in the binder.

Each week, go through the binder(s), and remove papers that no longer need to be transported daily to and from school. You may want to remove these papers during the weekend, since many teachers give children important papers for parents on Friday.

1. Sort the papers according to subject.
2. Go through each subject pile, and file the tests/quizzes into the correct folders in the file box.
3. Sift through the remaining homework and class work papers. Throw away papers that are not needed for homework checks, for teacher requirements, or as study tools for future exams.
4. File the saved papers under Class Work/Homework.

Summary

Throughout this book, we've tried to give alternative strategies to help parents find organizing solutions for their children. In our practices, we have had children who have tried different techniques before they found the one that worked for them. Asking your child questions and acutely listening to the answers will give both of you the information you need to design a new strategy together.

Here's the basic game plan to work from as you follow the paper trail:

- The child writes down the assignment, using a planner, Post-it wallet, or electronic document. Now she knows what to do.
- The child double-checks that the assignments are correct by having the teacher or a school buddy check the planner, using the class website, or calling a friend. Now she *really* knows what to do.
- The child places all materials touched that day into the Take Home section of the bifold. Now she has the correct materials.
- Daily, papers from the Take Home section are filed (into the binder or the file box) or put in that day's work pile. Now the child knows where the papers are. This is done under the watchful eye of a parent (at least in the beginning and then periodically).
- The child plans out the projects on a calendar, marking completion dates for each step of the process. These dates can be marked in the planner book, a regular monthly calendar, or a Post-it calendar. Now she knows that big projects are just a series of little projects. This "chunking" of the work keeps it from being overwhelming.
- When work is completed, it goes into the Take to School side of the bifold. A parent double-checks this. Now the day's work is put away correctly.
- Weekly, the backpack and binders are purged of papers that no longer need to be carried back and forth to school—they go into either that great trash can in the sky or the file box.

Now backpacks remain lighter, and when it comes time to study for tests, your child knows where everything is.

There; we just summarized a whole chapter into one page by asking the question "How can we reduce what we just read into as few key concepts as possible?" That technique of reducing information to the key concepts is part of the reading, note-taking, and studying methods that we'll explain in the next chapter.

Chapter 5

Super Study Skills

My Son's "Study Session"

My wife and I have divided study sessions with our son. She gets to review language arts and Latin with him. I get math and science. The day before our son had a biology test, my wife sent me to his room to check on his preparation.

"Okay," I announced cheerfully as I opened his bedroom door. "Mommy said I should test you in bio. Have you finished studying?" My son nodded and said, "Yes!" so I asked innocently enough, "Where's your material?"

My son looked at me as if I were from outer space. "What material? What do you mean?"

"You know, I need to see the stuff you studied, so I can test you on it."

"You can't see it. It's on my computer."

"Well, let me see the printouts you studied from."

"You can't," my son replied. "The notes are all over my hard drive and, well, I couldn't actually find them to print them out."

"What about the My Documents subfolders that I set up for you at the beginning of the year? It was so logical." I was very proud of that system.

"That system may work for you, Dad, but that's not the way my mind works."

"So," I said, "you haven't studied from your notes, have you?"

"Not really."

"Okay, so let's go to your textbook. I'll test you from there," I said. And there was my poor child, thumbing through his bio textbook, looking at it as if he had never seen it before. Even though we had bought him his own copy, there were no underlined sections or handwritten notes. In short, my brilliant A+ son couldn't take productive notes, didn't know how to get information from his textbook, didn't even know how to gather his materials together, didn't have a clue how to study, and hadn't asked himself any questions about the material. It was going to be quite a night. Mom was going to freak.

The Big, Powerful Concept: Question Everything!

Underlying reading, note-taking, and study skills is a simple yet extremely powerful technique: Ask questions! Have your child question everything!

Have your child ask:

- What did the teacher just say?
- What did I just read?
- Why is that so? Is it true?
- Where have I seen information like this before?
- How is this different from material I've previously learned?
- How can I summarize this in as few words as possible?
- How can I visualize this in pictures or flowcharts?
- What else do I need to learn about this?
- What questions about this are likely to be on the test?

And the big questions:

- Why is this important to me and the rest of the world?
- So what?

Bishop Mandell Creighton said, "The one real object of education is to leave a person in the continual state of asking questions." As Adam Robinson concludes in *What Smart Students Know,*

"Merely listening to the teacher and completing assignments is never enough." Asking questions and recalling the answers—that's where the learning payoff comes in, since no one can teach you like you can teach yourself.

> Ask questions! Question everything! This simple yet extremely powerful technique is the key to learning!

Reading Effectively: Ask Questions

Let's start our chapter on study methods with reading skills. The SQ3R reading technique was first developed by Dr. Francis P. Robinson in 1946 and has withstood the test of time. We've simplified these steps of effective reading in the following box.

Effective Reading Technique in a Nutshell

1. **Survey** the material. Look at the introduction, headings, pictures, sidebar information, bold words, conclusion, and summary.
2. **Question** what is coming up. Convert all of the text's headings into questions. (For example, turn the title "World War II" into "What was World War II?")

3. **Read** the text and continue to ask questions.
4. **Recite** or write down the answers to the questions you've been asking while reading.
5. **Review** all your material.

See the figure below for a visual representation of this technique. The immediate recitation of material (step 4) is an essential step in forming long-term memories. Without it, half of the information is lost within a day according to the Muskingum College Center for Advancement of Learning.

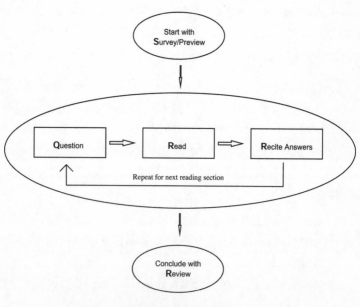

How to read effectively.

Start by teaching your child the SQ3R reading and Cornell note-taking techniques. They are simple, quick, and effective!

Taking Notes Effectively: Ask Questions

There are lots of different note-taking systems. They, too, are all based on actively asking questions such as "What are the key ideas?" and "How does all of this information fit together?" Our favorite note-taking technique is the Cornell system, developed originally by Dr. Walter Pauk at Cornell University.

The Amazingly Effective Yet Simple Cornell System of Note-Taking

Looking for a really simple method of note-taking for your child? Here's the Cornell method. It provides more than just notes; it also provides a ready-made set of materials to study from effectively. It's all so simple that your child might actually do it! Start with this technique, and get fancier with the additional methods as needed.

The Cornell Note-Taking System in a Nutshell

- Have your child draw two lines on a regular piece of notebook paper (page 101): a vertical line about two inches from the left edge of the paper, and a horizontal line about two inches from the bottom of the page.
- The big right section is for taking notes during class.
- The smaller left section is for writing down keywords and/or questions, to be done within twenty-four hours of taking the notes.
- The bottom section is for a summary and/or key questions about the page, also to be filled out within twenty-four hours of taking the notes.
- The material should be reviewed weekly.

A few pointers on the Cornell method to share with the student:

- Leave lots and lots of space between ideas. This provides a visual separation of topics and allows room for other information to be merged in later.
- If using loose-leaf paper, use only one side of the paper—it's easier to spread out the notes. Sorry, trees. We'll recycle at the end of the year.
- Avoid using full sentences when taking notes. Use abbreviations such as those in the table on pages 103–104.

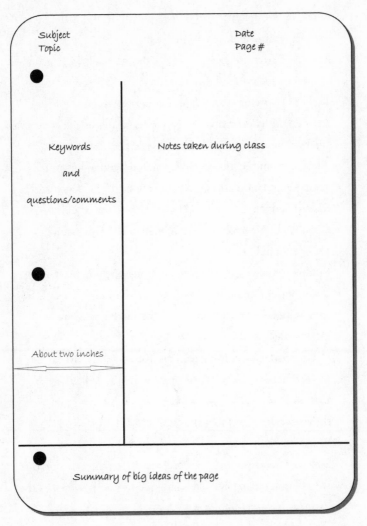

Preparing the paper for Cornell notes.

- Use the left column to reduce the information to the fewest possible keywords—keywords that can be used as hooks to recall/hang the information.

- Use the left column also to ask questions about the corresponding material on the right.

- Use the bottom section to write a summary of the page or ask some big, meaningful questions, such as "Why does this matter? How does this relate to other information I have learned? Why is this the case? What are the big ideas that are likely to be on the test?"

- Mark the notes with asterisks, colored highlighters, circles or other shapes, and arrows to make connections between the facts. For example, in history class, highlight all of the Republican presidents in red and all of the Democratic presidents in blue.

- Study by covering the material on the right. Look at the questions and the keywords on the left, and use those words to prompt recall of the covered material. It's like having instant flash cards!

- Recite the answers using explicit words—don't just fake it.

- Review notes each week. According to Walter Pauk's *How to Study in College,* students who do so will retain the material so well that they will ultimately save on study time.

- Some students put the keywords/questions directly into the left column during class, a technique formally known as the "two-column method."

Some common abbreviations for note-taking.

ABBREVIATION	STANDS FOR
p.	page
w/	with
w/o	without
b/c	because
+ *or* &	and
mo.	month
yr.	year
e.g. *or* ex.	for example
i.e.	that is; in other words
b.	born
ca.	about, around (stands for "circa")
diff.	different
lbs.	pounds
?	question
Δ	change
∴	therefore

ABBREVIATION	STANDS FOR
→	"leads to" (e.g., hunger → eating)
←	"comes from" (e.g., eating ← hunger)
↑	increase
↓	decrease
≈	approximately
≠	"does not equal" or "does not mean that"

See page 105 for an example of taking Cornell notes on the following brief story.

"WAFFLES THE DOG"

Let me tell you about my dog named Waffles. You may wonder how he got his name. Well, my father had a stuffed animal named Waffles when he was a kid. Also, I just thought the name sounded unique. He's a small dog, and his fur has areas of brown, gray, and white. He has the biggest eyes, and his tongue is always hanging out. He's so cute! He's not the smartest dog, though. When we got him from the breeder, we gave him the PAT—the Puppy Aptitude Test. He failed it terribly. He also took forever to be paper-trained. Even so, Waffles is the best dog ever: He's loyal, warm, fluffy, and soft, and he loves me!

English
<u>Waffles the Dog</u>

January 21, 2009
P. 1

●

Name

Named after father's stuffed animal
Name is unique

Looks

He appears:
    Small
    3 colors: brown, gray, white
    Big eyes *
    Tongue hangs out*

Dumb

Not the smartest
    Failed the PAT (Puppy Apt. Test)
    Slow to paper-train

● Lovable

Lovable b/c
    warm, fluffy, soft*
    loyal, loves author

* What does
Waffles have in
common with my
dog?

● Waffles has unique qualities like his name, eyes, and tongue. Like most dogs, though, he is soft and loyal.

Intelligence is not the most important quality for a dog. Is intelligence the most important quality for humans?

Example of Cornell notes based on the story "Waffles the Dog."

Now, here's another story ("Michael the Video Game Fanatic") for your child to use as a practice example for making his own Cornell notes. Go ahead and have him do it. It will only take a few minutes. Maybe you can negotiate his reward for doing a good job!

"MICHAEL THE VIDEO GAME FANATIC"

Michael loved video games: He loved the constant action, the amazing graphics, and the challenge of getting the highest score. His parents hated the video games, though. They thought some of them were too violent and that Michael spent too much time playing them. The fighting over video games was terrible. There was yelling and hurt feelings. One day, a simple solution was found. Michael could play thirty minutes per day on weekdays and an hour a day on weekends. If only everyone could learn how to negotiate!

Outline Form of Notes

As always, the subject, date, and title and page number (if applicable) go on top of the page. Explain very simply that:

* Roman numerals (I, II, III, etc.) are for major headings
* Capital letters (A, B, C, etc.) are for subheadings
* Regular numbers (1, 2, 3, etc.) are for important facts
* Lowercase letters (a, b, c, etc.) are for less major, related facts

Using the outline form forces students to search for the logic of the lecture (so it can be fit into the outline). Some kids, though,

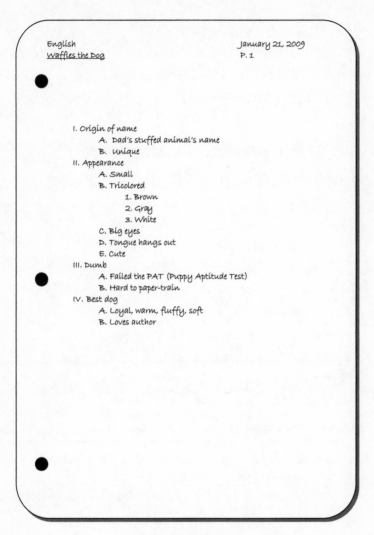

English   January 21, 2009
Waffles the Dog   P. 1

I. Origin of name
    A. Dad's stuffed animal's name
    B. Unique
II. Appearance
    A. Small
    B. Tricolored
            1. Brown
            2. Gray
            3. White
    C. Big eyes
    D. Tongue hangs out
    E. Cute
III. Dumb
    A. Failed the PAT (Puppy Aptitude Test)
    B. Hard to paper-train
IV. Best dog
    A. Loyal, warm, fluffy, soft
    B. Loves author

Outline form of notes.

might find this formal method frustrating and distracting. Of course, the child can modify this technique in any way that works for him. For informal outlines, a student might prefer to use "—" or "*" to start individual lines of information instead of the symbols above. See page 107 for notes on "Waffles the Dog" in outline form. Your child can practice the outline method using the "Michael the Video Game Fanatic" essay.

Visual Organizer Form of Notes

Visual learners may understand information better if they prepare a visual organizer. See pages 110 and 111 for examples.

Visual Organizers in a Nutshell

- Write the central topic in a bubble in the center of the page.
- Add lines radiating out from the central topic as new subtopics come up.
- Each new subtopic can then itself serve as a hub for additional information radiating out from it.

A Few Pointers on Visual Organizers
- Be sure to only write keywords and to leave plenty of room for new spokes.
- Some students start with the first subtopic at 12:00 and add additional spokes in a clockwise or counterclockwise fashion. Other students add the spokes more randomly.
- Some kids prefer writing the subtopics in a bubble, called the "bubble method" (see page 110). Others only have a central

bubble and write the subtopics along the spokes, called the "spider method" (see page 111).

- You can make the spokes between entries into arrows to indicate cause and effect. For example, "low blood sugar → hunger."
- Add little drawings to give visual meaning to the words. For example, put a smiling face next to something that is good or happy.

Have your child make his own visual organizer out of the "Michael the Video Game Fanatic" story.

How to Use Flash Cards

Flash cards are a great study technique, especially for paired information such as words with definitions, events with dates, English words with French words, and math problems with answers. Write the term or keyword on the front of a three-by-five index card and the answer on the reverse side. Keep the answers brief. See the example on page 113.

A Few Pointers on the Use of Flash Cards

- The learner should state the answer to herself out loud before turning the card over to check the answer.
- As individual cards are mastered, they can be set aside, allowing for more focus on the remaining difficult ones.
- Visual learners can use graphics on the cards.
- Use colored flash cards to distinguish genders in languages: pink cards for feminine words and blue cards for masculine words.

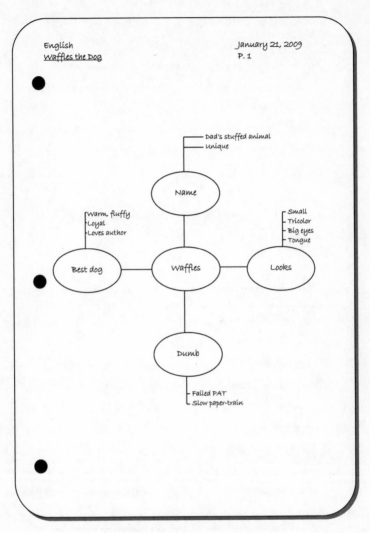

Visual organizer using the bubble method.

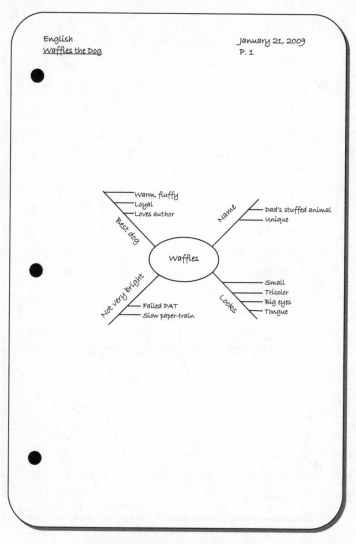

English
<u>Waffles the Dog</u>

January 21, 2009
P. 1

Warm, fluffy
Loyal
Loves author
Best dog

Name
Dad's stuffed animal
Unique

Waffles

Not very bright
Failed PAT
Slow paper-train

Looks
Small
Tricolor
Big eyes
Tongue

Visual organizer using the spider method.

- Note that the Cornell method actually provides study materials similar to flash cards, except the information can't be continually sorted like it can with flash cards.
- File the flash cards in a box when finished with them, as shown on page 43.

How to Underline or Use a Highlighter

Show your child how to underline or highlight key information only, not the whole sentence or paragraph. Mark the answers to the questions "Who, what, when, where, how, and why?" These answers will be the important information. Also, use two different colored highlighters if your child is working with subtopics within one major topic.

When taking notes, leave lots of space to visually separate topics and to allow room for additional ideas.

Additional Ideas for All Types of Notes

Here are some general suggestions for students that apply to any note-taking technique (see *Test-Taking Strategies and Study Skills for the Utterly Confused* by Laurie Rozakis and *School Power* by Jeanne Schumm for more ideas):

- On the top right of each page, write the date and page number (if applicable).
- On the top left of each page, write the subject (e.g., Social Studies) and topic of the day's lecture (e.g., The Pyramids) (see page 101).

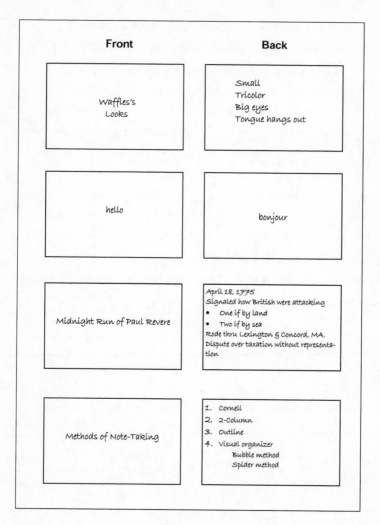

Flash cards.

- Always ask questions while taking notes. This turns students into an active listener and helps keep kids from falling asleep during class. Teachers will appreciate this!

- Put a question mark next to information that isn't understood. Your child can ask the teacher or another student to clarify. Don't wait until the night before the test to address the issue!
- Preview the reading material the night before the subject is covered in class. This will make classroom note-taking easier. If the teacher follows the textbook closely, your child may be able to just add further comments from the teacher to his textbook notes.
- Clues that something is important enough to take notes on:
  - The teacher writes it on the board.
  - The teacher takes a lot of time to explain it.
  - The teacher emphasizes it, repeats it, or says, "This is important."
  - The teacher asks questions about the material. These will likely come up on the exam.
- Special accommodations for note-taking might include:
  - Use of a laptop.
  - Obtaining a copy of notes from the teacher or a peer.
  - Use of a scribe to write the notes for child.
  - Use of graph paper to help line up math problems.
  - Use of a tape recorder (but who has the time to listen to the whole lecture again?). Remember that you always have to ask the teacher's permission to use a tape recorder.
- Personalize the techniques with anything that works for you.

Study Effectively: Ask Questions

Billy is very proud. He has done all of his reading and taken notes. He feels that he is finished. It's time for a reward, like playing a video game. Mom keeps reminding him about the test on Friday, but it's only Tuesday; there's plenty of time left. Fast-forward to Thursday night. After countless arguments with his mom, Billy finally sits down to study. After all, the test is tomorrow.

Billy spends fifteen minutes clearing off his desk and turns to finding all of his notes. Where are they? They've got to be in here somewhere! And where's his iPod? He can't study without his iPod! Forty minutes later, Billy has all of his materials together—well, except for his textbook, which he forgot to bring home. Although he hasn't reviewed a single fact, this study session is over. He's ready for a break.

Congratulations! Your child has read all of the material and taken good notes. Now he's ready to study for the test. Perhaps surprisingly, many students don't know how to study. Some never had to study; some were never taught. Here are some high-yield suggestions for fast, effective study.

Get All of the Material Together

Your student can't study if he doesn't have something to study from. It sounds so basic that we shouldn't have to say it, but this step is a huge hurdle for so many kids. So, the first thing is to get all of the material together. If you've followed the strategies in chapter 3, this should be a piece of cake—the material is either in his binder or in his file box. Don't forget to gather handouts, flash cards, textbooks, or any other study materials.

Plan Out the Study Schedule

Plan out with him when he will use these materials to study. Use the monthly calendar to write out his study schedule. Leave plenty of time. Expect the unexpected.

Note to parents: Some people rely on the proximity of the test to get themselves to finally study. They just *can't* bring themselves to study or work today on a paper that is not due until next week. Only an imminent deadline can get their attention. It's certainly not ideal, but it may be the way it is.

Buff (or Rewrite) Your Materials into Effective Forms for Study

Once your child has taken good notes and you've shown him how to get all of them in one place, what's next? Auditorily inclined students will benefit from having someone test them on the material as if they were taking an oral exam. But many students—especially visual learners—need to be sure that their notes provide an effective visual study aid.

- If your child has used the Cornell method, he has already taken notes in a form that lends itself to study. Just have him cover the right-hand column and ask himself questions based on the left-hand column keywords. He needs to say/write the answer out loud, whisper it to himself, or "hear" the answer in his head using explicit words, then double-check himself by uncovering the material on the right.

- He may find it useful to rewrite his notes utilizing one or more of the techniques in this book—such as visual organizers, outlines, or flash cards. (Not every kid has the patience to do this—if you are reading this, your kid probably doesn't! Just make sure he at least uses the Cornell method for taking the notes.)

....

As your child buffs his study materials, he should merge to-gether information from his textbook and his class notes. He needs to keep coming up with new questions!

....

- While revamping his notes, he should combine class materials with information from the textbook. (That's one of the reasons he left plenty of room when he wrote class notes.)

- He should keep coming up with new questions and associations, ask how things are related (or different), keep marking notes with new comments, and color-code corresponding material. For example, he could underline in green all of Waffles's good qualities and underline in red all of his negative qualities. Perhaps he could put arrows between statements to show their relationship better. Help him make the notes meaningful to him. It is the "Aha!" moments of new associations—when the lightbulb goes off—that are the most fun and satisfying!

- He should make up study sheets after each topic is covered, combining the material from several lectures if possible. Teach him to ask himself, "How can I organize this information so it makes the most sense in the fewest words?"

> The act of trying to reduce the major concepts to just a small space will help him understand the crux of the material.

- As he understands the material better and better, the review notes will actually become shorter and shorter. We promise you. Major topics should take no more than a page! From a few key ideas or diagrams, he can figure out all of the rest.
- The act of trying to reduce the major concepts to just a small space will help your child's understanding of the material. The process of making the review sheets is the "heavy lifting" part of his studying. Now he really understands it. Committing to memory material that he really understands is much easier and almost automatic. Once you have the larger framework, it's easier to keep track of the smaller facts.

Use Study Buddies

Studying with friends is a great way to study—after your child has already learned the material on her own. Be sure she brings all of her study materials with her.

✓ AUDITORY LEARNERS really benefit from hearing their study buddies.

✓ CHRONOLOGICAL LEARNERS, though, might prefer studying the material with their own techniques and logic.

Point out to your child that study buddies provide a great way to:

* Come up with questions she wouldn't have thought of on her own.
* Be sure that she uses explicit words to clarify her answers.
* Find out if she really understands the material—before the test!
* Learn about material she doesn't understand. She should ask her friends about anything that she doesn't understand. This is not the time to fake it! (If she doesn't fake understanding now, she won't need to fake understanding during the exam.)
* Have someone fill in material she missed.
* Have fun while studying.
* Eat chips.

Taking the Test: Strategies that Really Work

Has anyone ever taught your child how to actually take a test? Probably not. It's a shame not to get the best result possible on the exam—especially after all of that hard work everyone did preparing for it. Here are some test-taking strategies to maximize scores, adapted from *Teaching Learning Strategies and Study Skills to Students with LD, ADD, or Special Needs* by Stephen S. Strichart and Charles T. Mangrum; *Middle School Study Skills* by John Ernst; and *Essential Study Skills* by Linda Wong.

Time Management During the Test

Smart test-takers manage their time during the test by using the following techniques:

- First, she turns over the sheet and writes down all keywords, dates, formulas, or phrases that she has memorized for the test. Now she doesn't have to worry about forgetting them.
- Then she looks over the test quickly to see what's coming up.
- Next, she reads the directions carefully! Some kids do better if they are taught to underline the keywords of the directions. (If nothing else, at least the adults can be sure the child read them.)
- See which questions are worth the same number of points, and answer the easier ones first. If a question is harder or lengthier than other questions worth the same number of points, she puts a large mark next to it so that she can see it and come back to it later.
- Leave a question mark next to answers that were guessed at.
- Sometimes the answer to one question is contained elsewhere on the test. That's another reason to skip difficult questions and come back to them at the end of the test.
- Sometimes she might be able to ask the teacher for help. She has to be subtle here, but try asking the teacher:
  - "Can you rephrase the question?" That may result in a clue.
  - "Am I interpreting the question correctly?" The teacher should tell the student if her interpretation is correct or not.
- If there is time at the end, check the answers. Look for careless mistakes. Cover old answers when trying the question again. Only change an answer when really sure that the new answer is correct.
- When unsure, guess (unless there is a penalty for wrong answers).

True/False Questions

When taking a true/false test, use the following strategies:

* Look for clue words.
  ○ A statement is usually *false* if it includes absolute, all-or-nothing, or black-and-white words such as "every," "never," "always," "all," "only," "should," or "would."
  ○ A statement is usually *true* if it includes moderating or qualifying words ("shades of gray") in the answer, such as "most," "some," "usually," "might," "may," "seldom," "sometimes," or "some."
* Longer statements are frequently true.
* A statement is only true if *all* of its parts are true.
* Outrageous or ridiculous statements are usually false.
* Don't read too deeply into the sentence.
* If the student has no clue, guess "true."

Multiple-Choice Questions

* Read the question and try to give her own answer before reading the listed answers.
* Then read the question along with each choice.
* Be sure to read all of the listed answers! Don't just choose the first answer that seems right!
* Cross out the clearly incorrect answers. This is particularly useful for those kids who just can't wait to start making marks on the paper.
* Often the longest, most detailed answers are correct.
* "All of the above" is likely correct if you are sure that at least

two of the answers are correct or if "all of the above" has not
been a choice in most of the other questions.

- If left with more than one possible answer, the first choice is
  usually the correct one.
- If the answers are all numbers, the right one is probably *not*
  the highest or the lowest.
- As a last resort, guess "C." This seems to be the most
  common teacher choice for the correct answer.

Be sure to read all of the listed answers! Don't just choose
the first answer that seems right.

Fill-in-the-Blank Questions

- Read the question, thinking about the answer.
- If different blanks are of different lengths or the questions use
  differing numbers of blanks, then the teacher is giving a clue.
- If there is an "an" before the blank, the answer has to start
  with a vowel.
- If unsure of the spelling, pay attention to see if it is printed
  elsewhere on the test.
- The teacher may give partial credit if the student describes
  the answer, even if she can't recall the exact term.
- After writing in the answer, read the entire sentence. Does it
  make sense?

Matching Questions

- Read all of the items in both columns before starting. If one
  of the columns is a list of long definitions, start with one of

them. After she reads the definition, scan for the answer in the other column. This technique saves time since she is not reading the lengthier definitions over and over.

- Start with the matches you are sure of.
- Cross out the answers once you use them. (But check the directions: Sometimes an answer may be used more than once, in which case it can't be crossed off.)

Essay Questions

- Try to predict the questions in advance and set up an outline to answer each question during study time.
- Start with the easiest question first.
- Look for the key direction word that tells what to do, such as "summarize," "explain," "illustrate," "describe," or "compare" (show similarities *and* differences). Do what the directions say!
- Circle vocabulary words in the question that have been studied. Be sure to define them during the essay.
- Brainstorm ideas. Write them down on scratch paper or the back of the test. They don't have to be in any order, and the writer doesn't need to use all of the brainstormed ideas in the essay.
- Then, using the brainstormed ideas, make a short outline or a graphic organizer to plan out the essay.
- The introduction should state clearly what is being proved. This is the thesis statement.
- A single-paragraph answer should include the thesis in the topic sentence, several supporting sentences, and a concluding sentence.
- A multiparagraph essay should include:

- An introductory paragraph with a clear thesis followed by the major supporting points. Include keywords that are part of the question.
- Several (often three) supporting paragraphs, each with its own topic sentence and supporting statements. Keep each paragraph to one main idea.
- Transition phrases (such as "As a result" or "Also") to link one paragraph to the next.
- A concluding/summary paragraph.

- Be sure to use and/or define some of the keywords or concepts taught during the section.
- Edit the essay. Don't repeat information or ideas. Say it right. Say it once.
- Use formal language, such as replacing contractions like "don't" with "do not." Throw in an occasional big word, as long as it is used correctly.
- Try to avoid beginning sentences with lengthy but noninformative phrases. For example, instead of starting with "I am going to explain the many reasons that I like biology, such as," use "Biology fascinates me because . . ."
- Be neat! There's no credit if the teacher can't read it.
- If running out of time, submit an outline. The essay may still earn partial credit.

Math Tests

- Before the test, be sure to have studied:
  - Facts, such as definitions and formulas.
  - Procedures, such as how to add fractions. Practice

procedures by *redoing* problems from the notes or from the textbook. Don't just look over your previous answers—that's not enough!

- Remember to write formulas on the test paper as soon as possible to avoid getting nervous and forgetting them.
- Solve the easiest problems first.
- Show all of the work to get at least partial credit.
- Never leave an answer blank. At least show beginning steps.
- Check work as each step is done. Look for careless mistakes as one goes.
- Later, if there is time, reread and do the problems over in a separate space.
- In word problems, look for keywords that tell you what math operation to use. In particular:
  - "of" means "times." For example, "½ *of* 6" means "½×6," i.e., 3.
  - "is" means "equal." For example, "the sum of A and B *is* 5" means "A+B=5."
- Label your answers. For example, when asked to calculate the time a task will take, don't just write "2"; write "2 hours."
- Ask "Does this answer make sense?" For example, if the answer is "It will take the baker 2,184 years to make the cupcakes," the answer doesn't make sense!
- Use graph paper if your child has trouble lining up the numbers in your work.
- Ask to use additional paper if your child needs more room to show your work neatly. The typical test paper doesn't provide nearly enough space for many children to logically show their work in sequential order.

- After getting the test back, learn how to do the missed problems correctly—or the problems will keep following your child on future work.

Good luck to everyone!

Summary

Asking questions is the key to effective learning.

Effective reading, like all learning, starts with asking (and answering) questions. The reading technique called SQ3R (Survey, Question, Read, Recite, and Review) is based on this active learning process of asking questions. Start by Surveying (previewing) the material. Make a mental map of where you are going, and lay out some questions to answer. Then, section by section, ask Questions, Read, and Recite (and/or Record) the answers. A quick way to come up with questions is to turn headings into questions. At the end, Review all of the information.

Effective note-taking also requires asking questions. The Cornell note-taking technique divides note-taking paper into columns and has the child take notes in the larger, right-hand column. At home, he asks what key concepts can serve as hooks/cues for the rest of the information. These hooks are written next to the corresponding material in the left column. At the bottom of the page, he summarizes the material. Other note-taking techniques include outlines (formal or informal), visual organizers (bubble or spider method), and flash cards.

Take the class notes and reading notes and buff them into a brief review sheet. Forming these sheets, which involves synthesizing the material into as few key concepts as possible, is a great learning technique. Study buddies may also be helpful.

Test-taking techniques include writing down key formulas at the start of the test so that they are not forgotten, planning out time, reading the directions carefully, eliminating wrong answers, showing the work (even if it's just partial work), and carefully checking the results—but trusting one's first instinct unless sure that the answer was wrong.

Chapter 6

The Morning and Nighttime Routines

"Oh, to have my child get up in the morning without a fight would be a blessing! I have to call up to her at least four times, but she still can't get out of bed. Needless to say, by the time she gets out of bed, dresses, and has eaten a bite of her breakfast, the bus is already here. She barely makes it."

In our initial consults with new patients, we ask parents and children to describe their morning and nighttime routines. The parent and child inevitably will pause and look at each other as if to say, "Are you going to tell her or should I?" It's truly almost humorous to watch this nonverbal communication transpire while we're sitting there, already knowing the answer to our question.

Believe it or not, disorganized children can be disorganized even regarding when to go to sleep and when to wake up. You're probably sitting there shaking your head either in agreement or in disbelief. Just think about it—they can't even go to sleep or wake up effectively on their own! Here are some questions to ask yourself:

In the morning:
- Do you have to call your child's name repeatedly to get her up?
- Once she's awake, does it take a long time for her to get out of bed?
- Is she wasting time looking for items in the morning?
- Does she go back into her room after breakfast, never to be seen again?
- Is she late for school, the bus, or friends picking her up?

At night:
- Does your child get everything set for the next day?
- Does your child take a long time to get ready for bed?
- Does your child give you a hard time about going to bed?
- Is your child up late at night?
- While in bed, is your child doing something else other than sleeping?

Chaos occurs for the disorganized child if there are no strategies in place for the morning and nighttime routines. We've already organized the daytime and early-evening study hours. It only makes sense to extend the organizing strategy to all waking hours. Such structure will help disorganized children thrive throughout the day.

The Morning Routine

Too many parents struggle with their child's morning routine. The child cannot get out of bed, cannot find her clothes, has no idea where her homework is, and routinely has to be driven to school because she missed the bus. The parents are frustrated, along with the child. In fact, all the household members are affected by the morning arguments, even if they're not directly involved. Mom is yelling at Tommy that he needs to get dressed quicker, Tommy can't find his shoes so he's yelling for someone to help him look for them, and his sister Kathy has a knot in her stomach because of all the turmoil in the house. Everyone starts off the day completely stressed out. Who needs this in the morning?

Getting Her Out of Bed in the Morning

Probably the most common challenge that parents have in the morning is getting their child out of bed. There are some children who can arise bright eyed and bushy tailed, but a great number of parents who seek our help have children who are members of the "Just five more minutes!" club—and don't always request those five minutes in the nicest fashion. Five more minutes turns into fifteen more minutes in bed. These fifteen minutes delay the morning rituals, usually resulting in the child being late for school.

START THE MORNING PROCESS THIRTY MINUTES EARLIER Some children simply struggle with waking up and getting out of bed. For them, their actual bedtime (or amount of sleep) has no effect on the waking process. One of the strategies we recommend is to start the morning thirty minutes earlier. Some of you are probably frowning at this advice, but in the long run it may be worth it. If your child requires more time to transition from the sleep stage to the waking stage, this should work for you.

Try waking the child up thirty minutes earlier. It takes the pressure off, and it really works!

GET AN EFFECTIVE ALARM CLOCK Some parents complain that alarm clocks don't work for their child. Their children sleep right through the roaring alarm. These children are in such a deep sleep that the only thing that works is the parent coming into the room to physically awaken them.

In our experience with alarm clocks, we have found an assortment of fine (albeit somewhat dastardly) instruments that meet the needs of most heavy sleepers. Our favorite is the Clocky, the runaway alarm clock. It is unique in sound, shape, and function. When the alarm sounds, the clock not only makes an unusual beeping and chirping noise, but it also vibrates. It can jump off the nightstand onto the floor and roll around. To turn off the alarm, you have to get out of bed and scoop up the Clocky, which is bouncing on the floor. There are some other clocks, such as the Screaming Meanie and the Sonic Boom, that set off an obnoxious high-decibel sound that would wake anyone up. The Sonic Boom also vibrates and has a flashing light as part of its armamentarium.

For the child who really needs to get out of bed to be completely awake, there are clocks that require the completion of multiple tasks in order to shut off the alarm. Jigsaw puzzle alarm clocks explode pieces of a puzzle out of the clock and require your child to put the pieces of the puzzle together correctly before the blasted thing can be shut off. This will certainly get your child out of bed and moving in the morning. (You can find all of these clocks easily by searching the Internet for the name of the alarm. Include the words "alarm clock" in your search.)

For those who do not want to spend money on another alarm clock, consider an old clock radio. Place the clock radio on the other side of the room, and set the alarm to play a type of music that your child does not like. We worked with a child named Paul who didn't seem to respond to his clock radio. We found out that Paul had set his alarm to the music station he enjoyed. We asked Paul what type of music annoyed him the most. It was classical. We suggested that he set his alarm to a classical music station. Well, the look on Paul's face made us realize that this switch in music just might be the answer. The following week, when we checked in with Paul and his mom, they were surprised by how well the strategy worked. This technique can be used with an iPod alarm clock. Just download some music that your child doesn't like.

Establishing Morning Routines

Establishing morning routines will create order in your child's life and will help your child get out of the house in time to make the bus. Your child will start the day off with less stress, more confidence, and a backpack full of all the items she needs for school.

USE PICTURE CHARTS FOR YOUNGER CHILDREN For younger children, you may want to use a chart with pictures to depict the tasks he needs to complete. If you want your child to brush his teeth, comb his hair, and then get dressed, help him to cut out pictures of a toothbrush, a child combing his hair, and a shirt and pants. Place the picture of the first task at the top, and follow with the other pictures in a sequential order. Do not overload the chart with pictures. Keep it simple. Remember the saying "Less is more."

USE LISTS FOR OLDER CHILDREN For older children, discuss with your child the tasks that need to be accomplished in the morning. Begin with the moment your child gets out of bed. List the main tasks that need to be accomplished before she eats breakfast. For example, after Jackie gets out of bed, she washes her face, brushes her teeth, and puts on her clothes. Sometimes you may not have to list such basics. When Jackie comes downstairs she should be completely dressed and have all the belongings that she needs to bring to school. There should be no reason for her to go back upstairs to her room. If your disorganized child runs back and forth to her room to look for things she left behind, she will be there forever. Keep your child where you can see her! Do not let her go back into her room—it is a black hole. Jackie will eat breakfast; get her backpack, which is by the front door; and get on the bus for school. Trust us that you will have a winning solution if you can keep your child out of her room in the morning.

Once your child leaves her room in the morning, she shouldn't go back! Keep your child where you can see her!

PUT A LIST OF ACTIVITIES IN THE KITCHEN FOR TASKS TO BE DONE OUTSIDE OF THE BEDROOM You may also want to post a list in the kitchen of tasks that still need to be accomplished once your child is out of her room in the morning: put lunch in backpack, bring gym shorts on gym day, bring phone and keys, etc. This list will provide an additional reminder of all the items she needs for school.

> If your child has issues with eating breakfast, give him a breakfast bar on the run. If you're not a stickler for eating at the table, you might want to let him eat a small breakfast in his bedroom.

The Nighttime Routine

"We used to run around in the morning, looking for homework, sneakers, one glove . . . You name it, we couldn't find it. We spent so much time fighting about how these items should have been packed already that we would lose our focus, forget what we were looking for, and ultimately miss the bus."

Creating a system for organizing school items at night will result in your child feeling confident and responsible as well as less stressed in the morning.

The nighttime rituals start in late afternoon or at night, whenever homework is completed. Think about the tasks your child attempts to complete in the morning that result in her being late. Is she trying to collect all the items that need to be placed in her backpack? Is she trying to find her sneakers? Is she spending an enormous amount of time deciding what she is going to wear to school? These are common scenarios of the morning household rush hour.

Prepare the Backpack at Night with Tomorrow's School Material

Okay, so how do you start the nighttime routine? As we just noted, this process needs to start after your child has completed her homework. All materials that need to go back to school have to find their way into the backpack. Make sure that all homework due tomorrow is in the bifold. The child also needs to look at the planner to see if there is anything extra (textbooks, notebooks, etc.) that she needs to bring to school the next day. If so, pack it up.

We have great conversations with parents and children about where to keep the backpack. Younger children do not usually give their parents a hard time about where it should be placed. Therefore, you can place a younger child's backpack by the door she uses to leave the house in the morning.

Older children have many more responsibilities with homework, tests, and projects and may need their backpack in their study area for longer. It's been our experience that as girls gets older, they like to keep their backpack close to them as if it were a purse. That's fine. However, they need to place the backpack in a spot where they will see it. The best spot is always by the front door; but, if they so choose, they can leave it by their bedroom door—as long as it works out.

Prepare the Backpack at Night for Tomorrow's Special Activities

What activities does your child have the next day? Gym? Football practice? Art? If he has an activity that requires him to bring an item to school that he usually doesn't, he needs to have it packed in or next to the backpack the night before. You might want to draw up a chart listing the activities for each day of the week. Post this chart in a popular area in the house, such as the kitchen. If you have more than one child, you might want to list the activities for your children in different colors so everyone can easily distinguish the lists.

Prepare Clothes for the Next Day

If you have a girl, this is the mother of all detaining moments— what to wear to school! (There's something to be said for a school uniform. If you wore them as a child, you hated the heavy wool, the knee socks, and the boring patterns shared by all. Ugh! However, as a parent, you can see the financial and emotional practicality of them.) The time spent waiting for your daughter (and, yes, some sons) to pick out an outfit for school could be equivalent to the time it takes to cook dinner. These heart-wrenching, agonizing decisions delay the whole morning routine.

Have a conversation with your child about this issue. Point out that this task has been taking too much time in the morning, resulting in her being late for school or being just on time without a moment to spare. Have her select an outfit the night before, including shoes, underwear, and socks, and place it on a chair in her room. The rule is that she cannot change her mind about her selection. She may freak when you suggest this part to her. Tell her that she should give it a try for one week to see if it helps with being prepared in the morning. This isn't a lifetime decision; it's just a decision to give it a try. By giving her a trial period, it still leaves her feeling somewhat empowered about the task. Children have difficulty when their routine is going to change but can be more accepting and willing to participate if the new task is given in increments and on a trial basis.

....

Children (and parents) are more willing to try something new if they are asked to consider it during a trial period.

....

Don't laugh, but some of the children we work with have come up with their own solution to get out of the house on time: They sleep in their clothes. It's quite funny when the child discloses this fact and the mother sits there shrugging her shoulders as if to say, "I know it's crazy, but it works." The mother is right. If the child decides to sleep in his clothes for the next day, who is he bothering? No one. Have the attitude "So what? If it works for him, it's fine by me. It's not like he's sleeping in his snow jacket, hat, and gloves!"

Try to Have Your Child Bathe at Night

Another chore for children is hygiene. Most children will take their bath or shower at night, but as they get older, they may prefer to shower in the morning. Keep your child bathing at night for as long as you can. This is an activity that can delay the morning process tremendously, especially if your child likes to take long showers and has to blow-dry her hair.

Some children will fight you on the suggestion that they should switch this activity to nighttime. Children, especially disorganized children, do not have a good sense of time. What seems to be ten minutes to them is actually thirty minutes. If your child swears that she can take a shower and blow-dry her hair in twenty minutes, time her and show her the results. Chances are she took longer than she expected. Explain to her that if she wants to shower and blow-dry her hair in the morning, then she will have to wake up earlier. If the shower took her thirty minutes, then she needs to get up thirty minutes earlier. The other option is to shower at night and sleep in for an extra twenty to thirty minutes. It's a simple choice: sleep in or a cold morning shower. Develop strategies *with* your child. It's all about listening and compromising.

Summary

As always, ask questions (and listen to the answers) to determine what the problem is, and seek win-win solutions with your child. Consider the following suggestions. They may be easier to accept if offered on a trial basis.

The Morning Routine

- Wake up thirty minutes earlier. This simple technique really helps.
- Use effective alarm clocks that are annoying or hard to turn off.
- Establish morning routines with lists. (Use picture charts for younger children.)
- Once the child leaves her room, she should not go back—or she may never be seen again.
- There may be an additional list in the kitchen (for reminders such as "Pack lunch," "Bring jacket," etc).
- Consider a breakfast bar so your child can eat on the run.

The Nighttime Routine

- Prepare the backpack with tomorrow's necessary papers and books. Put all work to be brought back to school into the bifold.
- Prepare the backpack with tomorrow's special supplies, such as gym clothes. A written list of special supplies for each day of the week may help the child do this on his own.
- Prepare clothes the night before.
- Try to keep the child bathing at night.

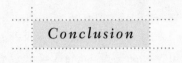

Conclusion

Congratulations!

You've made it to the end of this book. Hopefully, you and your child are all revved up to get organizational and study skills under control. It all really just boils down to a few principles.

If disorganization has been a roadblock to success, then you must teach and supervise some simple organizational skills. A straightforward and therefore doable set of techniques involves:

- Setting up a single binder or accordion folder for all subjects that has everything needed in it, so there is nothing to lose or forget.
- A Take Home and a Take to School section, either in a bifold folder or in the front of the accordion folder.
- A planner to record assignments. Back it up with the school

website, a buddy system in school, or a call to a friend from
home.

- A method to record the due dates of upcoming projects—
  either on a separate monthly calendar or in the planner book.
- A file box to unload papers.
- A surrogate frontal lobe, painlessly donated by a parent, to
  provide a safety net to ensure that the above system is
  actually maintained.

If poor learning skills have been the roadblock to success, then
we can teach a few simple skills. They all revolve around constantly asking questions and searching for novel associations
between the facts being learned. This makes studying more active, fun, and meaningful—and thus more successful. We've discussed:

- Effective note-taking with the Cornell method or visual
  organizers.
- Effective reading with the SQ3R method.
- Effective study techniques including a brief weekly review
  and reorganization of the notes, if helpful.

Some children just need to be shown these skills and they're
off to the races. Heaven bless them! Others—perhaps yours—are
waiting for further frontal lobe growth to kick in during later
childhood and young adulthood. Some children are more likely to
be on the fifty-year plan. They will continually work on mastering
these skills throughout their lives. Those who never become completely organized on their own will hopefully learn to accept the

loving help from those around them—family and associates. And hopefully, the family and associates will learn to gratefully accept the wonderful person with whom they have been dealt. There is a great person under there—not a perfect one (is there such a thing?)—but a great one. Organizational problems do not define a human being.

Throughout it all, remember that we're all on the same team. Everyone, from child to parent to teacher, wants the same thing: For the child to experience happiness. Now, by happiness, we don't just mean having fun. We mean happiness as a sense of gratitude, self-worth, and contentment—so much so that the child wants to go out and help other people achieve their own happiness. Such happiness is what adults want for the children who have been entrusted to their care. We may disagree on how to support them on the way, but we all share that common goal. Take home lesson: We may be frustrated with our children, but this isn't war against them. We're all on the same team, and the winner is the family in which the child still wants to come home.

No one said it was going to be easy. As M. Scott Peck begins his book *The Road Less Traveled*, life is difficult. Indeed life consists of a series of problems to be solved. We shouldn't feel surprised or "put upon" that we are facing some challenges with our children. That's life. It's happening up and down the street and around the world.

Meanwhile, this is the only time on this planet that we get with our children. Enjoy the ride!

Now, let's get back to the journey.

Could It Be Something Else?

If your child is truly more disorganized—and/or having more trouble learning—than most of his peers, it's worthwhile to at least consider if something else is going on. If disorganization is really the main problem, then Attention Deficit Hyperactivity Disorder may be the culprit, although learning disabilities, auditory processing problems, and depression and/or anxiety may also be playing a role. These problems frequently co-occur and can also be confused with each other. You can discuss these issues with your child's doctor, guidance counselor, school psychologist, or teacher. In some cases you might need a child neurologist or psychiatrist to help sort out the issues. Don't be afraid to be your child's advocate! Mothers, especially, are typically amazingly attuned to knowing that *something* is wrong.

Attention Deficit Hyperactivity Disorder (ADHD/ADD)

Attention Deficit Hyperactivity Disorder (ADHD) occurs in about 5–8 percent of children around the world. That's a lot of kids. It's not just for boys anymore; it occurs in plenty of girls as well. Frankly, many—if not most—of the children in our practices have ADHD.

According to the current *DSM-IV* criteria of the American Psychiatric Association there are two major categories of ADHD symptoms:

1. inattention
2. hyperactivity-impulsivity

In the inattention category, there are nine criteria. Four of them indeed refer to being inattentive or having a short attention span: Doesn't give close attention, doesn't sustain attention, doesn't seem to listen, and is easily distracted. However, the other five criteria all relate to organizational problems! These criteria include difficulty organizing, trouble following through with organization, avoiding activities that require organization, losing things, and being forgetful. Does any of this sound familiar? As we just saw, five of the nine criteria for the inattentive type of ADHD all relate to organizational problems—and you only need six of the criteria to diagnose ADHD of the predominantly inattentive type. In other words, if you are significantly disorganized, you are already ⅚ of the way toward a diagnosis of ADHD. (Conversely, you typically can't be diagnosed with ADHD unless you have to work at problems with organization.)

Then there are the nine criteria of the hyperactive-impulsive group. Six of those nine criteria relate to physical hyperactivity, such as being fidgety, being always "on the go," or talking excessively. The other three relate to impulsivity: blurting out answers, interrupting, or having trouble with turn taking. A child needs to meet at least six of these nine criteria to be classified as the hyperactive-impulsive type.

According to all of these criteria, three types of ADHD can be diagnosed:

1. ADHD, predominantly inattentive type. (Girls are more typically of this type, which was previously called ADD. These are the "Earth to Jill!" kids. In particular, bright, cute girls who are inattentive tend to slip by under the radar—until everything catches up with them in their later school years.)

2. ADHD, predominantly hyperactive-impulsive type. (This type is very rare: hyper but not inattentive.)

3. ADHD, combined type. (Both inattentive and hyperactive-impulsive types occurring together. This is the most common type.)

DSM-IV also adds a few other criteria to the diagnosis of ADHD, such as the symptoms should start before age seven, need to occur in at least two settings (such as school, home, or work), and need to actually interfere with a child's functioning.

Even more importantly, the current understanding of ADHD extends far beyond mere problems with inattention and/or hyperactivity-impulsivity (as if that weren't enough!). It includes problems with what are called "executive functions," the skills needed to:

- stop what you're doing
- remember what did and didn't work in the past
- look forward to your future goals
- talk to yourself about making a plan
- flexibly change the plan as circumstances change
- actually execute the plan

Again, we can see how many of these problems overlap with those of our disorganized students.

So how do we tell which kids have ADHD and which kids are simply disorganized? See the table below for some clues. If you have any concerns, discuss the issue with a knowledgeable professional.

Comparing simply disorganized children to ADHD children.

SIMPLY DISORGANIZED CHILDREN	SHARED CHARACTERISTICS	ADHD CHILDREN
	Disorganized	
	Trouble completing a plan	
No attention span problem		Attention span is short, except for fascinating activities, such as anything with a screen.

SIMPLY DISORGANIZED CHILDREN	SHARED CHARACTERISTICS	ADHD CHILDREN
Not easily distracted		Easily distracted
Not hyperactive-impulsive		May also be hyperactive-impulsive
Disorganization problems respond more readily to simple instruction		Disorganization problems tend to be recalcitrant to simple instruction
Mild overreactions, related mostly to schoolwork		May be very overreactive, not just to schoolwork
Milder effect on quality of life		More severe effect on quality of life

Learning Disabilities (LD)

Whenever a child is not living up to her potential, the possibility that she has a learning disability (LD) should be considered—especially when a child's aptitude for a particular type of task falls significantly below the rest of her skills. Common learning disabilities include dyslexia (trouble reading), dyscalculia (trouble with math), and dysgraphia (trouble with handwriting). Anyone who has a learning disability may have trouble mastering study skills, along with trouble completing work in a timely fashion. A learning disability by itself, though, does not lead to disorganization in other areas of life, such as the morning or evening routine. Learning disabilities are formally diagnosed by psychologists and educational specialists, who conduct a detailed psychological-educational evaluation. These evaluations are performed individually with the student and include IQ and achievement tests.

Central Auditory Processing Disorders (CAPD)

When we listen, sounds have to be converted into words, then words are converted into phrases, and phrases are converted into meaning. Children with a central auditory processing disorder (CAPD) have trouble somewhere in this process of converting the sounds that enter their ears into meaning. Although their reading comprehension might be normal, kids who have a CAPD have trouble understanding what they hear—especially in a noisy room. This makes them particularly prone to difficulty following oral directions, which may make the students appear disorganized. Actually, their organization skills are fine; they just never heard the directions correctly. Of course, a student might have both CAPD and ADHD.

Anxiety and Depression

People who are either anxious or depressed are frequently subsumed by their worries or sadness. Subsequently, they may have trouble concentrating and completing their tasks—and thus may appear disorganized. Anxiety is marked by strong, multiple, frequent worries that occur well in advance of the feared activity. For example, it is normal to be worried about tomorrow's test, but if your child is worried about Dad getting home safely, and about a wolf eating your dog, and about the SATs coming up in two years, that's an anxiety problem. Depression in children may manifest as sadness, withdrawal, giving up, loss of interest, or maybe even just irritability. Problems with sleep and/or appetite are frequently markers of both anxiety and depression. Often, no one knows about any of these problems unless the child is asked directly. So ask!

Further Resources

General School Supplies

The Container Store: www.thecontainerstore.com
K Mart: www.kmart.com; 866-KMART-4U
Office Depot: www.officedepot.com; 800-463-3768
Office Max: www.officemax.com; 800-283-7674
Staples: www.staples.com; 800-378-2753
Target: www.target.com; 800-591-3869
Wal-Mart: www.walmart.com; 800-925-6278

Assignment Planners

Success by Design: www.successbydesign.com. We
   particularly like Success by Design model 2045D.

Locker Supplies

Book Checker: www.thekidorganizer.com

Locker Mate: www.lockermate.com; 800-322-4332. Maker of locker supplies to buy in stores.

Locker shelves: www.stacksandstacks.com. Search "locker storage" to purchase shelves online.

Post-it Supplies

Picopad wallet: www.containerstore.com or www.thetravelinsider.info/travelaccessories/picopad.htm. Refill with three-by-two-inch Post-its.

Post-its: www.postit.com

Online Calendars

Keep and Share: www.keepandshare.com

Google Calendar: www.google.com/calendar. Can be set to text-message reminders to a cell phone.

Software

Software to control computer use: www.familysafemedia.com

Keyboarding and other educational software reviewed at and available for purchase from Kidsclick: www.kidsclick.com

Post-it software: www.postit.com. (Search the site for "digital
notes.") You can download the program for a free thirty-
day trial period.

StudyMinder has a free trial download at www.studyminder.
com. It features a simple homework organizer that keeps
track of work times.

Writing/visual organizer software: www.inspiration.com.
Download a free trial of Kidspiration software for grades
K–5 or Inspiration software for grades 6–adult.

Timers

Time Timer: www.timetimer.com. An easy-to-set visual timer
that shows a shrinking red wedge as the time expires.

Timers of all types: www.eadhd.com

Timers to control TV, video games, and the Internet:
www.familysafemedia.com. Stop the fighting over "screen
time" with devices and software from this well-designed
site.

Alarm Clocks to Awaken
Anyone or Anything

Sonic Boom clocks make piercing sounds, vibrate, and flash:
www.sonicalert.com

www.google.com and search for the "Shake Awake clock" or
"Jigsaw Puzzle Clock"

Homework Help Sites

Kidspace of the Internet Public Library: www.ipl.org/div/
kidspace. Has links to a wide range of resources such as
dictionaries and encyclopedias.

Math and Reading Help for Kids: www.math-and-reading-
help-for-kids.org

PBS Kids: pbskids.org

The Stacks (Scholastic's website for kids): www.scholastic
.com/kids

Time for Kids: www.timeforkids.com

Yahoo! Kids: www.kids.yahoo.com/learn

Organizational Skills

Franklin, L. (2003). *How to Get Organized Without Resorting
to Arson*. California: Cara Fyer Books.

Gold, M. (2003). *Help for the Struggling Student*. San
Francisco: Jossey-Bass.

Goldberg, D., and Zwiebel, J. (2005). *The Organized Student*.
New York: Fireside.

Organization tips for all aspects of life: www.lifeorganizers.com

Teaching organizational skills: www.addadhd.suite101.com/
article.cfm/teaching_the_adhd_child__part_1

Information for visual-spatial people: www.visualspatial.org

Zentall, S., and Goldstein, S. (1999). *The Homework
Workbook: A Seven Step Family Plan to Hassle Free
Homework*. Plantation, Florida: Specialty Press.

Study Skills

EKU Teaching and Learning Center: www.tlc.eku.edu/tips/
    study_skills

How to study: www.how-to-study.com

Luckie, W. R., and Smethurst, W. (1998). *Study Power.*
    Manchester: Brookline Books.

Robinson, A. (1993). *What Smart Students Know.* New York:
    Three Rivers Press.

Rozakis, L. (2003). *Test-Taking Strategies and Study Skills for
    the Utterly Confused.* New York: McGraw-Hill.

Parent Support & Educational Consulting

STARFISH Advocacy Association: www.starfishadvocacy.org

Coaching

To find coaches: www.addcoaching.com and
    www.edgefoundation.org

National Association of Professional Organizers:
    www.napo.net

Education Groups

National PTA: www.pta.org

National Education Association: www.nea.org

Neurobiological Conditions

Attention Deficit Hyperactivity Disorder

ADHD: 101 Tips for Teachers: www.dbpeds.org/articles/detail
.cfm?id=31

Additude magazine: www.additudemag.com. Search for
articles pertaining to organizing children.

Barkley, R. A. (2000). *Taking Charge of ADHD: The
Complete, Authoritative Guide for Parents*. New York: The
Guilford Press. Dr. Barkley offers groundbreaking
material on the nature of ADHD and executive functions.

Children and Adults with Attention Deficit Disorder:
www.chadd.org. Reliable information and support
groups.

Hallowell, E. M., and Jensen, P. S. (2008). *Superparenting for
ADD: An Innovative Approach to Raising Your Distracted
Child*. New York: Ballantine Books. This new book
emphasizes the positive aspects of a relationship with a
child who has ADHD.

Hallowell, E. M., and Ratey, J. J. (1995). *Driven to Distraction:
Recognizing and Coping with Attention Deficit Disorder
from Childhood Through Adulthood*. New York:
Touchstone.

Kutscher, M. (2008). *ADHD: Living Without Brakes*. London:
Jessica Kingsley Publishers.

Learning Disabilities

LD Online: www.ldonline.org. A superb resource including
   fair, full-text, useful articles on multiple issues.
Learning Disabilities Association of America: www.ldanatl.org
National Center for Learning Disabilities: www.ncld.org

Childhood Behavioral Problems

American Psychiatric Association. (2000). *Diagnostic and
   Statistical Manual of Mental Disorders,* fourth ed. (text
   revision). Washington, D.C.: American Psychiatric
   Publishing. The "official" U.S. diagnostic criteria for
   mental disorders.
Brooks, S., and Goldstein, S. (2001). *Raising Resilient
   Children.* New York: McGraw Hill Publishers. Wonderful
   book for all parents.
Kutscher, M. L., Attwood, T., and Wolff, R. R. (2005). *Kids
   in the Syndrome Mix of ADHD, LD, Asperger's, Tourette's,
   Bipolar, and More!: The One Stop Guide for Parents,
   Teachers, and Other Professionals.* London: Jessica
   Kingsley Publishers. Dr. Kutscher's book on the full
   syndrome mix of conditions that often accompany ADHD.
Dr. Kutscher's website: www.KidsBehavioralNeurology.com
Greene, R. W. (2005). *The Explosive Child.* New York:
   HarperCollins Publishers. This a must-read for parents of
   inflexible-explosive children who do not respond well to
   typical reward systems.
National Dissemination Center for Children with Disabilities:
   www.nichcy.org

References

American Psychiatric Association (2000). *Diagnostic and Statistical Manual of Mental Disorders,* fourth ed. (text revision). Washington, D.C.: American Psychiatric Publishing.

Barkley, R. A. (2000). *Taking Charge of ADHD: The Complete, Authoritative Guide for Parents.* New York: The Guilford Press.

Ernst, J. (1996). *Middle School Study Skills.* California: Teacher Created Resources, Inc.

Franklin, L. (2003). *How to Get Organized Without Resorting to Arson.* California: Clara Fyer Books.

Greene, R. W. (2005). *The Explosive Child.* New York: HarperCollins Publishers.

Kutscher, M. (2008). *ADHD: Living Without Brakes.* London: Jessica Kingsley Publishers.

Peck, M. S. (2003). *The Road Less Traveled, 25th Anniversary Edition: A New Psychology of Love, Traditional Values and Spiritual Growth.* New York: Touchstone.

Muskingum College Center for Advancement of Learning, Learning Strategies Database, "SQ3R Strategy." www.muskingum.edu/~cal/database/general/reading.html#SQ3R, referenced 2009.

Pauk, W. (2001). *How to Study in College,* 7th ed., Boston: Houghton Mifflin Co.

Robinson, A. (1993). *What Smart Students Know.* New York: Random House, Inc.

Robinson, F. P. (1946). *Effective Study.* New York: Harper and Bros.

Schumm, J. S. (2001). *School Power.* Minneapolis: Free Spirit Publishing, Inc.

Strichart, S. S., and Mangrum, C. T. (2002). *Teaching Learning Strategies and Study Skills to Students with LD, ADD, or Special Needs.* Boston: Allyn and Bacon.

Tullos, R. *Vocational Preparatory Instruction: Staff Self-Training Program,* Learning Styles Module. www.floridatechnet.org/inservice/vpi/assess/modules/Learning.pdf, referenced 2009.

Wong, L. (2006). *Essential Study Skills,* fifth ed. Boston: Houghton Mifflin Company.

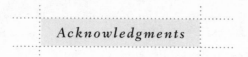

Acknowledgments

Behind every great team there is an even greater coach. Debbie Stier, our guide and editor, believed in our work and encouraged us to share our strategies with the world. Her inspiring enthusiasm made the arduous task of writing a book seem effortless. Her never-ending support and the continuing hours she poured into our book are small examples of Debbie's dedication to her work. We are forever grateful to Debbie and the entire staff of HarperStudio.

ERIC KUTSCHER

Martin L. Kutscher, M.D., is board certified in Pediatrics and Neurology, with Special Competency in Child Neurology. Dr. Kutscher is a graduate of Columbia University's College of Physicians and Surgeons. He completed his pediatrics at Temple University's St. Christopher's Hospital for Children as well as a pediatric neurology fellowship at the Albert Einstein College of Medicine. He is currently an assistant clinical professor of Pediatrics and of Neurology at the New York Medical College and maintains his own medical practice of more than twenty years that is currently limited to pediatric behavioral neurology. Dr. Kutscher lectures internationally and is the author of several recent books, including *ADHD: Living Without Brakes* and *Kids in the Syndrome Mix of ADHD*. Visit him online at www.SyndromeMix.com.

GILBERT KING

Marcella Moran, M.A., L.M.H.C., is a licensed psychotherapist and educational consultant who works with families to develop positive strategies for students who are disorganized. Her unique skill of assessing a student's learning style with an organizational style has proven to be a successful strategy for developing personalized organizational systems for students of all ages. While serving as coordinator for the Counseling and Psychological Services at Fordham University's Tarrytown Campus in New York, Moran has helped students gain self-awareness and to improve academic performance through individual and group counseling. She has made presentations at numerous workshops and seminars on various topics, including organizing the college bound student, time management for students, and study skills. Before starting her consulting business, Moran worked as a New York State licensed middle school and high school guidance counselor. In addition to her private practice, she is also an adjunct professor at Mercy College.

To book Martin L. Kutscher or Marcella Moran for a speaking engagement, visit www.harpercollinsspeakers.com.